JEANIE

out of the

BOTTLE

A MEMOIR BY JEAN WRIGHT

ISBN 978-1-55483-573-7 (trpb)
ISBN 978-1-55483-574-4 (e-book)

Cover art by Blue Eye Design.

For my sons Bruce Gremo, Roger Gremo,
and my granddaughter Nanda Gremo.

An eternal thank you to a dear friend Diane Rickwood
for hundreds of hours of typing and challenges.

Jeanie out of the Bottle.

I am 94 years old.

It has taken eight years to write this book.

I couldn't have written it until I had understood my parents' pain and struggle.

The contents are true.

Foreword by Diane Rickwood,
August 2024-08-20.

Jean & I met back in September, 2017. During early casual conversations, she was sharing snippets of her life which she was writing about in long hand. At that point, I offered to type her memories, making them easier to read, and there started an incredible journey documenting her life story since her birth in England in 1930 until the year she emigrated to Canada, 1952.

As each chapter unfolded, I became fascinated and engrossed in the personal history I was helping to create on paper, describing the many different life experiences of this remarkable child-teenager-woman which resulted in "Jeanie out of the Bottle."

I feel Jean is truly a survivor, both mentally and physically. She is certainly an inspiration to me in many ways, and a testament to the strength of the human spirit.

So now, if you, too, would like to get to know Jean in more detail, I encourage you to read on.

Thank you, Jean. I feel privileged to have been part of creating your memoir and will always treasure our many conversations.

Jean age 12.

Jean age 15

The Safe Years

1930-1937

Salford

Lived With Grandma Mendi

Jean Josephine Davis

Born: August 22, 1930, Salford, England.

Middle name after my Grandma Mendi's half-brother, Joseph, killed in W.W.1 Ypres – age 18.

Father: John Davis (Engineer-Musician) age 26, Salford.

Mother: Elsie Davis (nee Leah) age 18, Stockport, Cheshire.

Salford, where I lived until age seven.

My first memory was around age two. I was trying to turn the handle on a door which had a white lacy curtain on the top part of it. The door opened and I toddled in. I was looking at a shelf with many things on it. What caught my eye was a glass dome. I touched it and it moved. The something under it looked good and I stuck my hand into it and put my hand to my mouth. The next thing was a voice saying: "No, no" and a hand took mine and led me away. Later I was told what I had found tasty was icing on a cake.

My parents ran a small grocery store, but it closed within six months. The great depression was taking place and millions were unemployed. Soup kitchens and bread lines were the sustenance for the poor.

When the grocery shop failed my dad decided to go to London

and try his luck as a musician in a dance band. My mother left Salford with me and went to live with her eldest sister, Annie, who lived in Stockport, around 20 miles away. Annie had two small children and her husband. He was an unemployed brick builder. I was under two years old. Visiting Annie when I was fifty, she put me into the background picture of John and Elsie's meeting.

Sister Elsie was "flighty" as she put it and used to go off, unbeknownst to Grandfather Leah, to the dances at Stockport town hall. John had his own amateur dance band and it would travel around playing gigs (one night stands). Although he was black she fell in love. At that time she had been going out with a boy she had gone to school with since kindergarten. Granddad Leah found out about the two and invited them both to the house. Annie was there at the time and my mother was told to choose and she chose my dad. Granddad Leah didn't know what my dad looked like till he showed up. I am sure it was a heck of a shock. They were married in September 1929.

Whilst we were at Annie's I played with my baby cousins; neither could walk. Annie would sometimes place me on a stand at a wall and tell me to watch the trains go by. I was frightened and wanted to come down. We only stayed with Annie three months. I don't remember my mother, only Annie. She went on to say because of my mother's flighty behavior, she wrote to my dad informing him that he had better get his wife and child to London. She was not going to look after me whilst his wife galavanted around. She had enough problems of her own to deal with.

I don't remember the move to London. My one memory was of a woman giving me a load of bread to carry. Then she took it off me and lifted me up and put me in a square chair. She started to push me and I went higher and higher. I was frightened as I held on tightly. I was happy when she stopped pushing me and put me back on the ground and gave me the loaf to carry. I guess she must have been my mother.

The other memory was a man taking me to a dark, small room and sitting me on a toilet, then he left. I held on as long as I could then my bottom fell into the hole and I couldn't get up out of it. I was frightened and started to cry loudly. The man reappeared. I could only see him from the waist down as he lifted me up, laughing all the time. I guess this must have been my father.

London, I was told, only lasted a couple of months and then I was sent back to live with Grandma Mendi, my father's mother, who lived in Salford. I lived with her until I was nearly seven. I loved being pushed in a chair with wheels on when we went to the market. Sometimes I would hear her say to me: "Here comes Willie Gabadon." Willie was a short and thin man, and dark skinned, unlike my Grandma's skin which was white. They would chat for a while. Then, with a big grin (I knew what he was doing), his hand would go into his pocket and into my hand would go a coin to buy sweeties. I liked "Willie Gabadon."

It was many years later when I realized how poor we were. Grandma would give me a saucer and send me to the shop for a half-penny of tea. I would watch the shopkeeper put a spoonful of tea on the saucer and at the same time tell me not to drop it. Another incident was going into another shop for three sausages; two for Grandma, one for me. This particular time I decided to sit outside the shop and eat my sausage. With fear I saw Grandma looking for me. All she said was: "Dearie, you were hungry!"

At about four, I was introduced to death by Grandma who, in her way, felt this was a natural way of facing life. One day she took me by the hand and we entered a house up the street. The room, although full of people, was quiet. Still holding her hand, we went over to a window and underneath, lying on a table, was a tiny baby in a drawer. I knew it was a drawer because it had knobs on the front of it. When we left, Grandma explained there wasn't enough money for a coffin and a nice man would come later to take the baby away in a box.

When old Mr. Valentine who lived next door died, Grandma took me in with her to see him. He was covered with a white sheet and a beautiful white lace canopy hung over the bed. I peeked at him as I was sure he was asleep. There were crosses and pictures all around the room. My attention was taken by a glass bowl on a table. The bowl was filled with chocolates. When Grandma was talking to Mrs. O'Lara, I took one, then another, and ate them. Knowing it was wrong, I peeked again to see if Mr. Valentine was looking. His eyes were closed good. I didn't feel happy about what I had done, knowing that Mrs. O'Lara had been very kind to my Grandma after she found me as a baby in a cabbage on her doorstep. She gave me to her.

Up till then, I had only seen dead people. This memory is of a young, very pale girl who sat at the other side of an open window. When Grandma and I went shopping, Grandma would stop and chat with her. Soon the girl was lying in a bed. What was she doing lying in a bed so everyone could see her? She smiled as Grandma talked to her and I noticed that she plucked at her bedclothes with her fingers. I was a little frightened of her as she was so white. I thought she might be a ghost. One day the window was closed. "Where has she gone?" I asked Grandma. Grandma said: "Jean, she has died. It was a blessing. Her suffering is over." My introduction to death at an early age has held no fear for me.

School was different this year. I was about five. We wore navy blue knickers with a pocket to hold a handkerchief. Grandma still insisted I wear the white knickers which I had always worn. I wore them under the navy blue ones. I did not agree and one day I threw the white ones away. Much to my horror, the next day Grandma was at the school demanding to know why I had no white knickers on when I came home. The look on Grandma's and the teacher's faces scared me as I cried and admitted I had thrown them away. Surprise to me. Nothing was ever mentioned. Many years later, Grandma told me the dye came out of the navy blues and it wasn't good for my skin. She wasn't having any of that.

On my fifth birthday I had a party. We had jam sandwiches and chocolate biscuits. Three children came with unwrapped presents in their hands. One was a tube of toothpaste, another of Drene shampoo, but my favourite was an orange pencil. Grandma's was a small bucket, soap and my own scrubbing brush so I would help her. What a lovely day. I was happy.

Jean aged 5.

Twice I was very ill. With the measles I was kept in a dark room. This was to protect my eyes. Grandma would sing funny songs to entertain me. I enjoyed that. Then I had double pneumonia. All day and night Grandma put hot poultices on my chest and back. I threw up a lot. She would clean me and then give me mandarin oranges to eat. We both slept in the same bed. I used to peek at her when she was undressing. One night she said sharply: "What are you looking for?" I guess I was curious about what was under her many petticoats and vests. I never found out. I didn't dare peek again.

I was sent to St. Cyprious Church of England. At Whitsuntide I would walk in a parade to commemorate Jesus' ascension into Heaven. Grandma would dress me in a lovely white dress with a veil. I would have a necklace and carry a basket of flowers. At every street we would stop and sing a hymn. I really liked that.

At school I was chosen to be "Little Bo Peep." Grandma bought me a green bonnet with a ribbon. As I took it off after the play, the ribbon broke. Grandma will be cross. All she saidwas: "I'll sew it back." Whew!

My mind began taking in many things. After all, I was a big girl of five. The day that Gregory Whitehouse was killed by a horse and cart taught me to look both ways before I crossed the road. I had only seen one car on our street and that was when this man and woman came to visit Grandma. All I remember is they looked well dressed and she had a fur around her neck with an animal's head on it. I guess that was my father and mother.

At one end of Monmouth Street where I lived was the Manchester Canal. It had a huge brick wall in front of it. We kids would go down and watch the huge ships go by very slowly. We could see the seamen on the deck as they threw down sweeties to us over the wall and waved.

The other end of Monmouth Street was Odsell Lane. The lane was lined with cotton mills. Many times when I woke up early I would creep into Grandma's room and watch the women and girls (many no older than 12) make their way to the cotton mills to work from 6 am to 6 pm on the looms. Their clothes made them look like witches; dark skirts with black shawls draped over their shoulders and heads hiding their faces, hands clutching the loose part of their shawl around what looked like shapeless bodies. Added to this was the clump, clump of their clogs on the tarred blocks of the road. I watched them, fascinated. I would return to my small bedroom conjuring up all sorts of stories in my head. I would quietly close my door with the nail in it for my nightgown and climb over the chair into my single bed and look up at the large portrait of Queen Victoria keeping her cross eyes on me as she held a ball and a stick on her hands.

Looking back I thought I was born in the Victorian age listening to Grandma sing: "Soldiers of the Queen, my boys" or "Marching to Pretoria." She did sing other songs like "It's a sin to tell a lie" or "Red sails in the sunset." I asked her one day why it was a sin to tell a lie. It was years later when I understood her answer. "Jean, a thief is not as bad as a liar. A liar can hang you." Where did she get all these sayings from? "Keep your ears open and your mouth shut,

Jean" or "It's better to be an old man's darling than a young man's slave." All this under my belt before I was seven and holding my Grandma's hand. No wonder I was a quiet child.

There were some exciting happenings, like going to the pictures and seeing "Old Mother Riley." Grandma would laugh till tears rolled down her face. In turn I would laugh at her laughing. Not very often we went to Bellvue Park. Grandma would pack sandwiches, biscuits and bottles of water. When we were there she would buy us an ice cream. She always brought John Kabatas with us. John was four years older than me. His mother, Lizzie, shared the house with Grandma, along with her three other children, one being a baby. John kept an eye on me as Bellvue was an amusement park and it was easy to get lost. I really loved John. When he went to Blackpool for a day trip with the school, he always brought me back a stick of "Blackpool Rock" with the name printed on it. The last time he also brought me a small gold chain purse. It was the most beautiful thing I had even seen.

Lizzie had the front room to the house. I would often go and sit with her whilst she fed the baby. My Grandma more than once would say impatiently: "Lizzie, it's about time you took that baby off the tit." What does she mean? I would ask myself. Sometimes sitting watching Lizzie I would see little things creeping in her hair. Another time, sitting on the bottom step at the front door, and she standing above me, I noticed she had no knickers on. Her husband was a merchant seaman captain and was born in Japan. He, like my grandfather, was away months at a time.

Granddad Bass came home when his ship docked in Manchester. They laid the seamen off a ship and the men would either resign or try to sign on another ship. Granddad Bass was black and born in Ghana, West Africa. He was taken as a boy and worked in the bowels of English merchant ships.

Grandad Bass Mendi.   Grandma Margaret Mendi

I loved when he came home. He would drop his kit bag on the floor, reach in, and pull out sweeties for me. One year it was a lovely black doll with legs and arms that moved. I made up my mind I wasn't going to play with her like the other doll which I dropped and her head broke into a million pieces. Even though Grandma sewed a cloth head for her and put in big button eyes, I never liked her again. "Well," said Grandma, "what are you going to call your new doll?" We went through lots of names and finally she said: "Margaret, that's a nice name." Who was I to disagree? So "Margaret" stayed. Years later I found that my Grandma, who was called Maggie, was really Margaret. What trickery.

Another time when Granddad Bass came home he put something in Grandma's hand. She looked down and yelled: "Is that all?" and threw the whole lot at the window! I stood, speechless, watching and listening with no understanding till years later. Men on merchant ships spent hours in boredom, with nothing to do but gamble to pass the time away. These below-deck sailors earned meager pay. They were paid after the ship landed at port. Many were broke by this time and owed their wages on paper. I guess this was one of those times that Granddad Bass lost.

Granddad Bass had a full, hardy laugh which he used when I would creep up and blow in his ear. His colour was a deep warm brown, his eyes big, especially when he would roll them at me. One day he was standing on the top step at the front door and I was sitting looking up at him, his face looking outward and eyes fixed on a far-away place. He looked peaceful smoking his pipe. Some kids older than me came along, stopped, and pointed at him, at the same time making strange noises. I was too young to understand, but what I saw and heard I did not like. What a lovely soul he was. I feel that he'd had his share of suffering. I loved Granddad Bass and never wanted him to leave.

At such an early age, I really learned so many lessons from my Grandma, a lady born in a workhouse in Durham County to a fourteen-year-old rape victim. There were no cuddles and kissy, kissy from Grandma, but lots of care with a heavy hand in a velvet glove. At seven, I was traumatized when they took me away from her, but she was my foundation which carried me to this day, ninety four years later.

Variety of early experiences.

1937-1939

London W1

Lived with parents.

At almost seven years, I was old enough to see my Grandma was upset. Her constant sniffling and wiping her eyes were a giveaway. Just before bedtime, guiding me up the stairs with a candle on a metal plate to my small bedroom with its single bed, a chair and Queen Victoria looking down on me, she told me the next day my father was coming to take me to live with him and my mother in a big city named London.

"Why?" I asked myself. "I don't want to go to London." I had always lived with my Grandma as far back as I could remember. The idea of going to a strange place to live with this father and mother I didn't know was difficult for me to understand. I was aware of this man called "Father" because he sent me the "Beano" and "Dandy" comics wrapped up in brown paper and delivered by the postman, which made me feel important. I don't think I had ever met him. Sleeping that night was troublesome. I looked up but could see Queen Victoria and I shuddered. Then I hid my head under the bedclothes. I was afraid. When I woke up in the light of morning, I was still frightened. I didn't want to leave Grandma Mendi.

I was a quiet child and rarely asked questions, at least not then. I watched as Grandma packed up my clothes in a large case. I then followed her downstairs, suitcase firmly in her hand. We sat in the living room waiting, not saying a word. I fidgeted and stared at the suitcase. I panicked; "Where's Margaret?" I ran upstairs to fetch her. Grandma suddenly smiled, gave me sixpence, and told me to go to the shop and buy Snakes and Ladders. "What were Snakes and Ladders for?" I asked. "To take with you on the train" was the answer. "Train, what train?" I said to myself as my tummy turned over. Saying over and over again: I am going to live with this father and mother I don't know. I don't want to know them and I don't want any Snakes and Ladders. I want my Grandma.

He arrived; tall, as I thought, light brown and with curly hair. He had a nice smile. He must be OK. Didn't he send me all those comics? My mind was whirling as I sat there looking at him whilst they both talked non-stop as though I wasn't there. "I am not going with him," I said to myself. Eventually, after we had eaten, he said:

"Time to go." I got up and meekly picked up Margaret. He took my suitcase as we walked up the passage to the front door. I was never asked if I wanted to go.

As we got to the front door, Grandma said: "Don't forget your Snakes and Ladders." "I don't want Snakes and Ladders," I said to myself. I picked the box up in silence. As we left, Grandma hugged me. I silently walked away with this stranger. I looked back to wave and saw something I had never seen before. My Grandma was crying. I bit my lip as we turned the corner, out of sight.

He spoke to me many times but I blocked his voice out of my mind. The train journey seemed to go on forever. I silently looked out of the window whilst sucking on my dolly's fingers, the Snakes and Ladders being pushed under the seat with my feet. I didn't want to see the box again.

London; we've arrived. I was quiet and sad as we pushed our way through the crowds of people. It was a long walk from King's Cross Station to where I was to live. As we walked he started to tell me that we lived in a flat (what was that?) at the top of a building. My eyes at this point were looking at all these tall buildings around me. I couldn't imagine living on top of one of those. I mean, how did we get up there?

My head was turning this way and that way as we made our way through the streets. People everywhere, going this way and that; lots of cars and big buses moving around. Then a whole new world opened as we turned a corner. A market: different sized barrows filled with fruit of all kinds; unusual smells filled my nostrils; pickles in barrels next to live fish in tubs. Coming out of the market, a woman badly dressed shoved a bunch of something at my father. He took it, gave her some coins, and she wished him a good life.

By the time we arrived at our street, my sadness was gone. I was excited by the hustle and bustle, and by everything I had just seen. He said, as we turned another corner: "Here we are, Gosfield Street, number 31."

The buildings were not as high as I had imagined. Some looked older than others, but they were joined together. Reaching 31, he said: "Look up at the top windows on the left … that is where you will live."

We climbed up eight flights of stairs to a landing with two doors on the right and two on the left. "Open the far door on the right, your mother is waiting in there" he said. I opened the door and facing me was a table, a chair and a fireplace. I could see no one. Taking a few more steps into the room, I looked to the left and there she was behind the door. She had red hair and was laughing. I held my breath. I had never seen anyone with red hair. She frightened me to death. I was afraid of her. This was my mother. It can't be!

It did not take long for me to lose my fear of her, but within a short time, I came to the conclusion that I didn't really like her. I soon became aware how much freedom I had, certainly more than I had at Grandma's.

My father had a dance band at the "Havana" nightclub. He left for the club at approximately 7pm, arriving home around 3am. Sundays and Mondays it was closed. As soon as he left, my mother would get ready and leave for the pub. I was familiar with the ones she frequented. I was instructed to play with the kids in the street and when it got dark to come inside, and then go to bed. The key was under the mat. Sometimes I would go looking for her. If I found her, a lemonade would be given to me and some money to buy chips; never enough for fish, just chips. Many times I would be in the street after dark. Then I would hold my breath and hightail it up eight flights of stairs, grab the key from under the mat, let myself into the flat, turn on the light, and jump under the bedclothes of the bed settee, which was already down. I would undress under the covers; that made me feel safe.

My father John Davis.

Havana Night Club 1937, Grandma Leah,
mother Elsie Davis, Auntie Phyllis.

I never knew if my father was aware of what was going on after
he left for the club. This freedom, after holding on to Grandma's
hand, was mind boggling.

It didn't take me long to settle down with the kids on the street.
They looked like the kids in Salford; clothes dirty, holes in their shoes
– just poor. I was the one with the three-wheel bike, scooter, skates,
nice clothes, etc. They didn't hold it against me. I was one of them.

Saturday was the big day. So many things to do. We all lived in
cold water flats, sharing a small sink and toilet with other flats. Any
of us who had the money (and I was one) would go early in the morning to the local baths, and for a penny would be shown into a small
room with a bath and chair, then the lady attendant supplied us with
a towel and a piece of soap and told us in no uncertain terms: "15
minutes, then out. No hanky panky." Little did she know.

One week when my friend Joan came with me, our bathroom was
separated by a room in between. The wall came part way up to the
ceiling. If we were careful, we could stand on top of the bath and
wave to each other and peep in to the other room between us. That
was my introduction to a naked body. It was interesting at times.
Sometimes Joan's eyes would meet mine and we would duck down
and giggle, stopping at "What's all the noise about?" from the attendant. It was no good staying in the bath longer than 15 minutes as

the voice yelled "Time" and the plug would lift and the water would start to drain out. Joan and I never spoke about what we had seen in the other bathroom. Naughty, I know, but we were only eight years old. If we wanted, we could always go to the other side of the building and, for another penny, swim for an hour.

The noise in the pool was deafening. We were given colored pins to wear. The old man who watched knew who had been in more than an hour. The kids used to give him the run around. He was really grumpy but I think he loved us, as he put our towels and swimming suits through the wringer.

After leaving the baths, we would make our way towards home through several side streets, all the time dodging men pushing racks of dresses and coats. This area was a clothing district once you had crossed over Oxford Street and were moving towards Mortimer Street.

More of we kids were ready for the best part of the day: The Tolmer Theatre, just off Camden Park Road. We were always waiting for next Saturday to come. We always went through the market to get to the Tolmer Theatre. We wouldn't miss the yelling of the costermongers, the colours of fresh fruit, the smell of fish, spices and perfume for anything. The market for we kids was a wonderland ready to explore.

My first stop was the cart of the old wrinkled man whose face resembled a tortoise. He sold perfume – "California Poppy," "Evening in Paris," – and also bright red nail polish, but best of all, Pond's Face Cream which the film stars used. He was a nice man. Sometimes he would dab some perfume behind some kid's ear. He squirted a boy one day who yelled out: "Blimey, now I smell like me mum!"

I would move on to the Indian. I knew he was Indian because he wore a turban. Round his neck was a coiled snake. He would ask us to touch it. We girls shied away. One boy even said: "Not me!" The beautiful silky cloth he had on his cart made you want to touch it. Our senses filled, we now turned to food.

I went to the Fish & Chip shop. The others went for jellied eels or eel pie. I couldn't even look at eels in green gravy or wobbling in jelly – ugh! Fish & Chips for me. Bellies full, off we went to, guess what, the Tolmer.

Being left in suspense by the serial the previous Saturday, we could hardly wait to see if the hero had been killed or had somehow escaped. It was always a mad rush as hundreds of kids pushed and shoved their way to the best seats. It was two pennies for all.

When everyone had settled down, loud banging and stamping of feet started, plus yelling for the picture to begin. There was a hush as the picture began with the serious news. When it was over, the laughing and jostling began. It could be "The Three Stooges," "Mickey Mouse" or "Donald Duck." If the noise was too much, a red faced man with a big nose would yell at us to be quiet. If the noise kept on, he would shout: "If you don't shut up, I'll knock ya bleedin' 'eds off!" We all laughed knowing he wouldn't do it … or would he?

The serial came on next with oohs and aahs as Tarzan faced all the dangers in the jungle. Every week it's the same. I'll always remember the moment when we approached the end of the serial picture. A lion is about to pounce on Tarzan as he in turn is about to rescue (Boy) his son from a man-eating tribe. Then those words: "To be continued next week." Hoots of disappointment and rage at having to wait another week to find out if Tarzan will escape the lion and save Boy from "a fate worse than death."

A "B" picture followed the serial. Nobody remembers it. The important thing is what's going to happed to Tarzen and Boy. Walking home through the market, our energy depleted, we started to look for broken fruit boxes which we would cart home and chop into smaller pieces, tie with string, and sell for a halfpenny to start the fire with. Or maybe a costermonger had a bruised peach for sale for a penny.

Roll on next Saturday. My parents knew the kind of day I had but never asked me about it. Bonding with my father was easy. He took care of my comforts, such as combing my hair to see if I had nits, giving me "Lickafruita" cough medicine, putting ointment on my scrapes when I fell down, and laxatives which I hated. The first time I was asked "Have you been to the bathroom?" I said: "Yes" – I didn't know what I was being asked. Sunday night he would put a basin on a chair in front of the fire and I would wash myself with water that was heated on a stove in a small closet with a window. He always washed my back and hair.

We went for walks in Regents Park and once we went to the zoo where I rode on an elephant and a camel. Having tea on the terrace of the "Houses of Parliament," but not as grand as tea at Hadley Woods. A band played music there while we had our tea of fancy sandwiches, scones and cream followed by lovely iced mini-cakes.

My friend, Phyllis Angel, was invited to come with us. We went to tea dances on a free afternoon. I would dance with my father. He would also dance with my mother who was a good dancer. I would take in all her moves.

There were times at the tea dance on Tottenham Court Road that the band leader, whom my father knew, beckoned me to go on stage to strut my stuff. Needless to say, I lapped up the applause from the audience; very heady for a seven or eight-year-old. He taught me many songs and would accompany me on the banjo or guitar. Every now and then, when their friends were in the living room, I was woken up out of their bed to sing a song or two. I never returned to bed without a few shillings. It was fun.

My mother would entertain their friends with a routine of "Popeyes." She shocked me when she took her teeth out and her chin would touch her nose. Also her "Charlie Chaplin" was very funny. She played the piano. One song was about "see the little piggies run with their fingers up their bums." I would hold my breath and try not to laugh.

One of her moments … I was walking home with Brown Owl when my mother appeared around the corner coming towards us. I was on edge. It was obvious she was a little drunk. I could tell by her unsteady walk. Reaching us she held out her hand and slurred: "Pleased to meet you, Brown Ale," then she started to laugh. Brown Owl never turned a hair. I stood, mortified. Over the years that yarn has produced much laughter.

The story I have kept under wraps … I came home from school to an empty flat. The pubs closed at 3pm so I went looking for her. Several times I had seen her disappear down the stairs of a building on Goodge Street. I made my way there. The room downstairs was packed with people drinking; lots of smoke and music. I couldn't see her and I went home. She was there. I told her where I had been. She crossed the room fast, yelling: "Don't ever go there again." Wham!

Her hand smacked my face so hard that I staggered back. No tears appeared. To my horror, she pulled me on her knee and tried to make light of the matter. Too late!

I feel that smack to this day. Never did cry, just stayed silent. My opinion of her was not high at this time. Red hair, hiding behind doors, no motherly expressions, less than funny songs, then that smack. What's a young child supposed to feel? Anger, hate, fear, confused, or all of them?

The next day my father told me I was going to a Christmas party and there would be lots of children there. I had a special dress. It had pretty smocking at the top and flowers around the hem. I was very excited thinking about it. We had to go in the bus to get there. It was in a huge building with lots of steps going up to the front door. A nice white lady with a fancy dress on came to meet us. She took charge of me saying: "You can pick her up around 4pm. What is your name, dear?" "Jean," I whispered. Taking my hand, she led me to the cloakroom where I left my coat. We proceeded into a large hall. There was lots of noise. My eyes riveted onto the tables which were covered with sandwiches, cakes, balloons and streamers. Next I saw the biggest Christmas tree I had ever seen. As the lady guided me to a chair with a bunch of kids around it, banging the table, laughing or moving around, I was surprised to see all the kids were different shades of brown. I briefly thought: "What am I doing here? I don't look like them."

Even though I was brought up with people who were dark skinned, I never thought I was like them. I was like my Grandma or mother: white. The thoughts left my mind as I dove into the yummy food with ice cream to follow. Afterwards, many white ladies guided us to see Father Christmas who gave us a present from under the tree. What a great party. The next morning, my father showed me a picture in the morning paper. The headline was: "Piccaninnies' Christmas Party." Once again I said to myself: "I'm not one of them and I'm not a Piccaninny." Because I wasn't. I am white. I established my identity there and then at age seven.

Life was moving so fast for me. Was it because my parents and I were dressed well, certainly not poor, that I was asked to do tasks by other people living in the street? I don't know.

Peg, who lived in a room in the basement, was one of those tasks. A lady from the blind school on Bolsover Street asked my parents "if I would like to escort Peg (who was blind) to the school each morning before I went to school. I said yes.

I never saw what was behind that dark, dirty outside door in the basement of the building in which we lived. As her door opened, Peg's lumpy body would fill the space completely, bringing with it a damp, musty smell. Facing me she would step out and close the door with her back to it. Turning her body around awkwardly towards the keyhole, she would poke a large key into the door, lock it, then drop the key into a brown tattered bag. Next she would adjust a well-worn hat before attempting to smooth wrinkles on an equally well-worn coat. She would then take my outstretched arm with one hand, the other being reserved for her white cane. Making our way to the foot of the stone staircase, we would begin the slow climb to the street above.

This daily ritual started at 8am, Monday to Friday. The first few minutes in which I picked Peg up were always scary for me. As a little girl of eight, I never felt safe until I was out of the basement well, and up on the street. I was paid a shilling a week to guide Peg to the Blind Institute on Bolsover Street, London. We would always take the same route. Walking slowly to the end of the street, we would turn left and proceed to the next corner on the way passing the newsagent's shop with its aroma of tobacco. With me looking both ways to make sure no horse and cart or motor car were coming, we would then cross the road, Peg's cane tapping steadily, and make our way in a straight line to the Institute. I would leave her at the back door and take off, heaving a big sigh of relief.

My eight-year-old body would then come alive as I ran, jumped and skipped my way to school. On the way I would stop off at the dairy for my fresh morning roll, my breakfast. The large man in the white apron always knew what I wanted as I thrust towards him the penny my mother had left for me. With a smile and a twinkle in his eye, he would cut a roll in half and put a large pat of butter with a cow stamped on the top. Once outside the shop, I would eat the dry half of the roll first. That way I could concentrate on the top half. I shall never forget the sensation in my mouth full of a soft roll and feeling the sweet butter trickling down my throat as it melted. Unfortunately, this morning routine was to come to a crashing end.

The morning before picking up Peg, I decided to water the flowers in the window-box of our fourth story flat above Peg's basement apartment. As I reached out over the window-box, the glass vase I was using slipped from my fingers. I looked down in time to see it about to hit a man passing below. Jerking my head away from the window, I heard a clang followed by a loud crash. Slamming the window shut, I ran down the eight flights of stairs to the street. Ignoring the commotion coming from the basement well, I ran all the way to school, Peg and my buttered roll completely forgotten.

During the morning, I did wonder what had happened to my mother's vase, however, by the time I arrived home for lunch I had forgotten all about it. That is, until I opened our flat door and saw my parents waiting for me, with grim looks on their faces. "I didn't mean it," I yelled. "The flowers were thirsty." They looked at each other, almost as if to laugh, then decided not to. In a severe voice my dad said, "The vase just missed hitting a man." It seemed the vase had missed the man and struck the railing before crashing through Peg's window, causing Peg to scream, "The Germans are bombing!" Continuing on its journey, the vase knocked Peg's fish bowl to the floor, then it hit the wall and smashed to pieces.

"What happened to the fish?" I whispered.

"They're dead," my father replied.

"I killed them," I said to myself. At that, I wet my pants and started to cry.

"I'm sorry, I'm sorry." My dad then assured me that we would go to Woolworth's and, with my pocket money, buy Peg another fish bowl and some more fish while he would pay for Peg's broken window. Needless to say, I could never look Peg in the face again and I resigned my job as guide for the blind.

When I came home from school, ladies would shout from their windows to me: "Jean, Jean, will you go to ....and buy this for me?" I would yell "yes" and down would be thrown money wrapped in paper, and off I would go on the errand knowing I would earn a penny or two.

One of these ladies was mysterious. She had a little baby, there wasn't a man around, and she never went anywhere. Her clothes were very fancy. Sometimes I would sit in her room as she checked what I had bought. So many nice ornaments and comfy chairs but best of all one wall was a mirror. It amazed me. The room looked twice as big. Then she moved away.

The other lady who I really liked … I always received a biscuit or chocolate plus a penny for my effort. The one problem was she kept me talking at the door about everything and anything. This day I'm standing and she goes on and on. She never noticed the pain on my face, the crossing of my legs. Then it happened! I wet my pants all over her door mat. I could have died with shame as she said: "Oh, Jean, why didn't you say you wanted to go to the bathroom?" I mumbled something then ran and hid myself. I could not face her again. After that, every time she called my name, I ignored her. She got the message.

There was only one lady whose name I knew; a Mrs. Stewart. Going to her basement flat was fun. She had a dog which would bark then lick me all over. I liked that. Before I left, she would always say: "Jean, would you like a biscuit?" I would answer: "I don't mind if I do." I agree she got tired of that answer. One day she replied: "For goodness sake, Jean, say yes or no." After that, it was "yes." She gave me two biscuits with a triumphant smile on her face.

There was one task I received nothing for except a nod of the head. On the first floor of the flats lived an old lady in her nineties. She would wait for me at her door. Her dress was black and she had a lace cap on her head. In her hand was a wooden handle with a hook on the end of it. She would beckon to me and I would take the hook and put it around buttons on her black boots, pull, and slip the buttons through holes on the other side of the boot. Her boots went half-way up her lower leg. When the weather permitted, she would sit looking out of the window to a world quite foreign to her.

I ran errands for a lady I wasn't comfortable with. This day instead of her shouting out of the window it was her husband. "Jean, will you go to the Home and Colonial for me?" "Yes," I yelled; why not? When I returned, I gave him the bag with the groceries. He put it down and said: "Come in." I went into the room expecting my reward. Instead he took my hand, led me to a chair and sat me on his knee. "This was not right," my mind said. Then he proceeded to put his hand up my knicker leg. Oh no, this is wrong. As I twisted, he looked me straight in the eye and I starred at him without a word. He stopped, took me to the door and told me to go, then the door closed behind him. I went home in shock. When I entered the flat, my mother was on her knees poking the fire. I bent down and whispered in her ear: "He put his hands up my knickers." She screamed, jumped up, dropping the poker. The look on her face made me laugh, which quickly stopped as I realized this was no laughing matter. "Who did this?" she asked, "and what else did he do?" I quickly told her everything, but she still asked: "Is that all?" "Yes, yes," I replied. Then she sent me down to play.

Coming home from school for lunch the next day, I opened the flat door and shrank back. "He" was there with his wife. Everyone was looking at me. "Come in," my father said. I moved in slowly towards my father's side. My eyes looked at the floor as my father asked me to repeat what had happened the day before, and I did. "Now, Jean," the man said, "that is not true. You have made it up." At that I burst into tears saying, "I did not, I did not!" My father told me to go and wait in the other rom. I did. I sat on the bed waiting for a long time, then my father called me in. They were gone, only my father and mother were there. My father put his hand on my shoulder and said: "I believe everything you said. Have some lunch then go and play." That's all I needed to hear. I ate a sandwich and chocolate bar and went out to play before I returned to school; everything forgotten.

I remember Mrs. Steadman. Her children were much older than me. I had a new dress on. I should not have worn it but I put it on without my mother's knowledge. Whilst at play, I tripped and the bottom of the dress was torn. Sitting on the steps crying, Eileen Steadman came along and when she knew my problem, she took me up to her mum who sewed it. It was like new. I wasn't sure of my mother's reaction to the torn new dress. Now I could go home. Whew!

There were so many stories around the flats. Christmas was approaching and my Auntie Phyllis and her friend were visiting from Stockport. I had money saved and I wanted to buy presents. This was going to be fun. Off I went to the market. I looked at gold bracelets, earrings that hung very low and perfume. I finally settled on what I was going to buy. Auntie Phyllis had a powder compact with a lipstick fixed into the end of it. Lucy, her friend, had a real pearl necklace. That was the most expensive gift. My father's gift was a large, red patterned scarf. I had seen one just like it on Mrs. Stewart's dog's neck. My mother's was a soft yellow dust cloth and a bright tea towel.

Christmas morning I was thrilled at the ooh's and ah's as I brought out each person's present. I was completely confused at the gails of laughter when I gave my mother hers. Then I made my way downstairs to the flat underneath ours. There lived a gentleman on his own. At times my mother and father would take me down and there would be other people there sitting around. When everyone was still, this gentleman would stand up and recite words and sentences. I didn't understand him, but he looked good. One time he said: "I shall finish with quotations from "Choo Chin Chow." That really impressed me. I was so impressed I bought him a lovely white handkerchief with a blue border. I gave it to him and he was overwhelmed. With lots of smiles he, in turn, gave me half-a-crown. Merry Christmas!

Opposite our two-room flat lived Nancy - she was four – who always wanted a ride on my bicycle. She couldn't ride it, so she would stand on the back step and hold on to my shoulders and I would peddle her around. This time to my sensitivity she farted loud. I stopped, told her to get off my bike, and took her up to her mother where I announced with indignation what she had done. "Nancy made a rude noise on my bike!" I turned as her mother smacked her legs. I left with great satisfaction. When my father came home, I told him about this shocking event. "She made a RUDE noise on my bike and she was smacked for it." The smirk left my face as my father sat me down and told me that was very unkind and I should be ashamed of myself. Then I got a lecture on why I had been unkind. He left me with my tail between my lets.

Playing on the streets was never dull. Siddy Brooks showed me how to let the tires down on a car. Get a long nail, put it into the area on the tire that lets air out, and voila! … tire flattened.

Because there was a car showroom in the next street, which was Great Portland Street, there were always cars to work on. The owner of the showroom, time and again, would approach we kids while we played and say: "OK, who wants to go to Primrose Hill to play?" We would pile into his big car and off we drove. On our way back home, he would buy us ice cream. We still let his tires down! Boo on us.

If we were bored, what could we do? Off we would go, over Great Portland, towards the posh part of London. We knew it was "posh" because maids or butlers came to the door after we rang the bell. We would say: "Please, can we use the toilet?" Most times they would tell us to "bugger off." If the owner came, we were often given coins. Then we would go and buy chips.

My thrill, because I had skates, was when the water truck, which cleaned the streets, stopped and I would then attach a rope to it and hang on for dear life. I had a bad fall with bloody knees as the result. It was my last ride.

The pleasant times happened in my 8th to 9th year. Two ladies, who were Jewish, asked me if I would come in and play with their daughter. One girl, Hesta, lived on my street. Her parents owned the three-story house. We would play "Ludo" and "Tiddly Winks" and read comics. Hesta and Jacqueline were not allowed to play on the streets. Their clothes, like mine, were nice. Hesta's mother would give us goodies to eat.

The yard we played in was overlooked by the big buildings around us. Jacqueline's was different. She lived in a large flat on Great Portland Street. Her room was beautiful with lots of toys, dolls and her own gramophone. Unlike Hesta, there wasn't a yard to play in. I didn't mind, her room was good enough for me. We would put records on and sing and dance to "Horsey, horsey, don't you stop, just let your feet go clippity clop" and "On the good ship lollipop." Her mother was glamorous. Also, chocolate cake and jelly donuts were her treats. Every so often Jacqueline's father turned up. He talked to me like I was grown up. When he left, he would put half-a-crown in my hand. I liked him. Later on, I was told his name was Michael Carr and he wrote songs.

There was great excitement at school. The older girls were talking about going to the Isle of Wight for two weeks' holiday with the school. This was to be in June. I wanted to go. I went to my teacher – her name was Miss Head (Daisy) – and asked her about it, then said: "I want to go." She explained to me that it was expensive and, also, I wasn't nine until August and I had to be nine-years-old. That didn't suit me. I went home and told my parents about it. The next thing I knew was my father telling me I was going. Not only that, but the next Sunday we were going to Heathrow to fly up in an aeroplane.

The aeroplane ride was so thrilling. I held my breath as I looked down at the little houses and fields. "Will he loop-the-loop?" I asked my father. "I don't think so," he replied, looking at my mother who was sick and very happy when we put our feet back on land.

The time had arrived to pack for the Isle of Wight. All my clothes, which were new, had to be marked with my name. I had to have two pennies a day to spend at the tuck shop, also a swimming suit and hat to swim in the sea. The sea! I could hardly wait! When we boarded the train, I had no idea that after the train ride we then had to board a ship to get us to the Isle of Wight. As I was the youngest on the trip, I kept close to the bigger girls, who were eleven-years-old. The ship was so much fun. Everyone was excited, even the two teachers who were with us, Miss Flynn and Miss Head. "There it is!" everyone shouted as we approached the Isle of Wight.

As we left the ship our teachers guided us to a waiting room until the bus came to take us to the Fairy Court where we were staying. We were shown around the building and grounds first, then we had supper followed by a trip to the tuck shop, and, finally, taken to the dormitory where we were to sleep.

I swam for the first time in the sea. It was salty. One day we found a large, dead rat on the beach. We dug a hole and buried him, then built a big castle over him. We marched around the castle singing: "Old ratty is dead and gone to his grave. Rah! Rah! Rah!" then we yelled, "Charge!" The older girls guarded the moat to prevent us entering the castle. The fun of it all!

We visited several other castles as part of our history lessons and education. I liked the dungeons best, also putting my legs and arms into the wooden stock. Other girls would then throw pretend fruit and vegetables at us.

I followed the older girls and tried to do everything they did. We spent half a day at Alum Bay filling egg timers with different colored sand. I brought mine home for my parents.

Some of the eleven-year-olds wrote a play about Persia. Everyone helped to put it on. We performed it the last day before we returned home. I played the part of a raggy beggar. I was told to cry in anguish: "Alms for the love of Allah!" I put my heart and soul into it. Then I ran off the stage being whipped. I was thrilled to bits!

That evening we were given the remains of our tuck money to buy something for our parents. I chose a box of jellied fruit.

Everyone was sad to leave "Fairy Court." The sail home was rough and some of the girls were sick. The parents met us at the station. My head went down as I sheepishly gave them their present of jellied fruit with several empty spaces in the box. I think their eyebrows went up and a knowing smile appeared on their faces as they thanked me. I just couldn't resist the temptation. How could I?!! I was only eight.

The last weeks at school went fast then I was packing to go for my holidays in Haswell Plough with my Great-Grandma Mary, Grandma Mendi and Great-Great Uncle George for two months. I would catch up with my friends. We would be blackberry picking, have picnics, walk for miles, and then sit under a haystack shaped like a house and tell stories.

Jean (9 years old) with Great Grandma Mary (65 years old)

Haswell Plough was so different from London, Fairy Court and Salford. It was quiet. Bedtime was 8pm. Home-made puddings and milk that came straight from the cow. It was a lovely summer until Peggy Donahue came rushing into the old stone house where we kids were playing and acting. She was shouting: "There's a war on! The Germans are coming! Jean Davis, your Grandma wants you home now. You're going back to London."

The mere word "war" made us all run. When I entered the house, my Grandma was already putting my clothes in the suitcase. Looking at my startled face, she said: "There's a war on and you're going back London tomorrow." I stood most of the way on the journey to London. The trains were packed with soldiers, sailors and airmen. I sat on my case, looking down on the label Grandma had pinned to my coat: Jean Davis, 31 Gosfield Street, London W1. My father met me at Kings Cross Station and we went back to the flat. Not a word was spoken.

1939-1944: WAR ON

EVACUATION – 5 years – lived with:

Mrs. Noctor – Mrs. Birdsey, Maple Grost, Rickmansworth, Hert. '39-40

Auntie Molly – Grandma Leah   '40-42

Grandma Mendi   '42-44

The next day, my mother took me to Marylebone Town Hall to receive a gas mask (this meant nothing to me). She told me a gas mask
was put over my head to protect me from gas poisoning which could
kill me. She also added that I, with all the children in London, would
be evacuated to the countryside till the war was over. (This also went
over my head.) Why couldn't I stay in Haswell Plough?" I thought.

Marylebone Town Hall was crowded with mothers, children and
babies crying; kids running in every direction. We were directed to
a man sitting surrounded by light brown square boxes. When it was
our turn to be served he beckoned us over, opened a box, and took
out a mask. It was black and had a window in front of your eyes. He
put it over my head, at the same time saying: "It's for protection in
case the Germans drop gas bombs from aeroplanes." He told me
never to go anywhere without it. "Keep it at the side of your bed
and if it gets damaged, have it repaired at the closest Air Raid War-
den's house." A lot to take in for a nine-year-old.

I now began to feel afraid as I looked around watching "Mickey
Mouse" and "Donald Duck" shaped masks being tried on younger,
crying children. There were also oblong boxes with windows in them
and a pipe coming out of the side; these were for babies. My mother
and I left with my name printed on the gas mask box.

The next day we went to my school where I joined my classmates
and we marched in a crocodile line to a railway station. I was clutching my dolly, a paper bag and my gas mask was slung over my
shoulder. The station was bedlam; mothers crying, children crying,
teachers scurrying here and there, giving orders as they put children
on the train. I noticed my mother wasn't crying. I boarded the train;
all I wanted was a window seat. Whoopee! I got one! I was very
quiet. Some kids acted like they were going on a holiday. The look
on the adults' faces as we steamed out of the station was a mixture
of tears and sadness. Also shouts of "Goodbye," "Behave your-
selves" and "I'll come and visit you."

Once we were on our way, the compartment noise stopped as we
made our way into the unknown. Every now and then, Miss Head
(Daisy) would slide open the door saying: "Everyone all right?" A
reassuring nod or "Yes" closed the door. Later on she popped her

head in again, saying: "Time for your brown bags; it's lunchtime."

The compartment came alive again with noise from kids discovering what their mums had packed for lunch. I opened mine and looked down, disgusted at soggy cucumber sandwiches. I waited till no one was looking then threw them out of the window.

It seemed hours before the train stopped. We were ordered to form a line and wait to be told what to do. "Jean Davis" I heard, before I found my class. I put my hand up and a nice lady with a pad and pencil in her hand said: "Come along, dear, follow me," which I did. I was crammed into a car with children I did not know. A long drive, then a voice said: "We're here now." I noticed the car had wooden sides. I had never seen a car like this. Later I was told it was called a "shooting break" and was used for hunting; hunting what? I thought.

A while later we arrived at a large house with a garden. We were told it was The Vicarage. We sat on the grass to wait for the people we would live with. Strange people coming for me. I didn't like that. I sat and sat, getting hungrier by the hour. My anxiety was increasing as name after name was called and these children left the garden. It was getting dark and there was only me and a little five-year-old girl still unclaimed. Finally, there she was, a nice-looking lady, looking for her two evacuees. Her name was Mrs. Noctor. I held the little girl's hand and off we went, relieved but frightened.

Mrs. Noctor's house was a council house, typical in design; two bedrooms up and two rooms down, with a bathroom squeezed in somewhere. Ushering us into the living room I sat with the little girl in front of the fireplace. I was very hungry by then. We were given something to eat. I can't remember what it was as my attention was riveted on a man who entered the room holding a baby in a basket. He introduced himself as Mr. Noctor. I was told the little girl was Norma. After we ate, Norma and I were shown our bedroom with one bed in it. Norma had still not spoken a word. The one thing that worried me - where is my suitcase? To my relief it was in the room next to a bundle which proved to be Norma's clothes.

Mr. And Mrs. Noctor, Jean, Norma and Vivian.

I settled down quickly. Miss Head was still my teacher and the school was only fifteen minutes away in Adswood. Where I lived was called Maple Grove. Each day we were given a drill about what to do when the air raid siren went off, and to know the difference with the "all clear." Even today, the sound of a siren sends shivers down my back. If the siren went when we were not at school, Miss Head would run up and down the street shouting, "Don't stand outside, get the children into the house." There were no air raid shelters built at this time. I remember having a bunch of people laughing at her and saying: "She's crazy!" Like many others at this time they thought it was a phony war. Little did they know what hell would rain down on us months later. Nobody laughed then.

Miss Head was a woman of her time. A product of the great W.W.1. A dedicated teacher and a mother to the forgotten. Many years later, I took my sons to meet her. Even in old age, she was spry.

Many children were left unvisited. Little Norma was one. She very rarely spoke. Just "Yes," "No," or a nod of her head. Being so young myself, I didn't understand what she must have been going through. She never cried, nor did I, but to my horror, I started wetting the bed and then, much to my shame, I heard Mrs. Noctor tell my father on one of his visits.

My father came often. I only remember my mother coming once

with a girlfriend. I never really missed my parents. It is hard to bond with parents who you have only lived with for two years, but I had a special place in my heart for my father. He had been the nurturer. My mother I observed with guarded interest.

Coming home from school one day I found Mrs. Noctor crying her eyes out. I was told Mr. Noctor had had a serious accident bicycling to work and was in the hospital.

Poor little Norma was sent off somewhere straight away. I never saw or heard of her again.

I stayed on and found myself sleeping in Mrs. Noctor's bed with her and the baby. She was afraid to be alone. I would be awake listening to Mrs. Noctor crying. I would worry I would wet the bed. A couple of weeks before Christmas 1939, my father came to visit and he told me Mr. Noctor was coming out of hospital and the family was going to Scotland, where he came from, to help him recover from his accident. They asked if I could go with them but my father said no. Two days later, off I went, carrying my dolly, suitcase and gas mask. I didn't want to leave Mrs. Noctor. I was very sad. I went to live with a Mr. & Mrs. Birdseye whose house was on the same street.

Mr. & Mrs. Birdseye met me at the front door. They had strong accents, which later I found out were Irish. This house was larger than the Noctors' with three bedrooms and a bathroom upstairs. I was shown to a small room with a bed, a chair and a cupboard with a mirror on it. My very own room! In the months ahead, I spent a lot of time in this room just thinking about myself. I was frightened. What was to become of me?

My life had been colorful enough. I spent many hours thinking (although I didn't know what the word meant). I started to look at my life in a philosophical way. I was aware that I wasn't comfortable in that house. It was clean enough, I was well fed, but I felt I was an intrusion. I couldn't make out what it was. I was getting a feeling that I was different, however, I didn't dwell on it. They had two boys, one three and the other six. It distressed me when I had to have a bath with them. I did not like it. I never said a word.

If I had any extra pocket money I would put it in a tin in the cupboard. I used to count it often. That's how I found out someone was pinching my money. I suspected Mrs. Birdseye had something to do with it. I never said a word. I did confide to my dolly, who was my best friend. I told her I didn't want to eat any chicken after seeing its neck wrung. This was the first lonely Christmas of many that were ahead of me.

Just before Christmas, Mr. Birdseye asked me to deliver a parcel to an address in Rickmansworth. I found the street and the house. This house was unlike any I had ever seen. It stood on its own with a garden and gate at the front. It had large windows on either side of a heavy dark door with a big brass knocker in the centre of it.

My timid knock was answered by a lady inquiring what I wanted. I told her and she invited me in and relayed my message to a man standing on a ladder hanging holly over glass doors. Immediately I found myself in a hall with wooden floors and patterned carpets on it. Both sides of the hall had glass doors leading to a room. One set of doors was closed, the other set, where the man was standing, was open. Glancing past him I could see a table with a variety of lovely Christmas decorations on it. At the end of the hall was a curved stair- case which also had boughs of holly tied to it. I had never been in a house like this.

As I was quickly taking all this in, the man came down from the ladder smiling and thanking me for delivering the parcel. Taking the parcel from me, he put his hand in his pocket and gave me a florin. As he showed me out, he wished me a "Merry Christmas." I was de- lighted with the florin but my thoughts were on the house. I told my- self that one day I wanted to live in a house just like this. It never quite happened but … almost.

My thoughts now began to focus on the school Christmas party. I wrote and asked my parents for something new to wear for it. A local friend, Jean Castle, told me about the one her mother was making for her. Mine was going to look every bit as nice as hers, I told my- self.

The parcel arrived. With great anticipation I tore it open and groaned at what I saw;   a dark brown sensible skirt with a top to match made, of all things, of wool. True, it had a few flowers on it and it was my size, but … it was not soft and silky. That, with my short frizzy hair and sensible shoes. I knew the party was going to be a flop. Needless to say I avoided Jean Castle like the plague; her with a white silky dress, a yellow sash and a matching bow in her hair. I could have yanked her long fair hair. She was still my friend until I stole a pencil from Woolworths and her mother forbade her to play with me again.

Life settled down to school classes. The one thing we looked forward to was the Saturday morning pictures. Hundreds of children would make for the pictures. Many of them were evacuees. We would sing our way to catch the bus into Rickmansworth. "Before we cross a busy road, what do we say? Look to the left and look to the right, and we'll never, never get run over." Once inside the cinema, we then sang, "We walk, never, never run as happily we go to the Odeon." We were happy, innocent children living in a comparatively protective and safe time. Were we really safe? From what?

This particular Saturday morning was different. My father was arriving on the 10 am bus. Quickly I washed and dressed. I still had to walk to the terminal where the bus arrived from Rickmanswworth. The double decker bus always arrived on the half hour, stayed fifteen minutes, then returned to Rickmansworth. I didn't want to be late. I always tried to be early. I didn't want to miss anything.

I was really early that morning, but in my pocket I had a lump of chalk with which I drew a hop scotch circle on the pavement. All I could think of was, "What's my father going to bring me?" He always brought me a surprise; chocolates with a picture on the box, comics or sweets. I was completely wrapped up in my own world when, slowly, I became aware of a black car stopping on the other side of the green. Mildly curious, but not stopping from jumping from square to square, I saw four men in the car looking at me. The back door opened and a tall man got out and came towards me. He stopped a little way from me and asked my name. I gave no reply and continued to hop scotch. I didn't like him. All the while the other men watched us. Feeling uncertain, I stopped and stood, stared at him. "Would you like a ride in a car?" he asked. I said nothing. At that moment I saw the bus coming from Rickmansworth. The tall man put his hand in his pocket and took out sixpence. "You can have this if you come for a ride," he said, glancing towards the car. He waited for what seemed ages, then he turned and walked towards the car. He stopped, put the sixpence on the ground and said, "Are you coming?" We looked into each other's eyes; I still said nothing. Did he see the bus? I don't know. He waited a moment, then turned and made his way back to the car. When I saw him get in, I ran forward, grabbed the sixpence, and ran as fast as I could to the bus approaching the pub, which was the terminal. As the bus emptied, the driver and conductor went off for a smoke. I immediately climbed onto the rear platform and watched the men in the black car drive away. I stayed on the platform until the conductor returned and told me to buzz off. I never told anyone what happened, not realizing that I had been in danger.

Once again I started jumping hop scotch, but this time I had a sixpence clutched in my hand. At last the bus arrived bringing my father, complete with a parcel under his arm for me. I can't remember what my "surprise" was because of the big news he had to tell me ... I was to leave the Birdseye house and move to Stockport in three weeks to live with my mother's sister, Auntie Molly, and Uncle Arthur. They had two girls I did not know. "Oh, no," I said to myself. "Not living with strangers again!" They were "family" but strangers to me. That thought faded as the five less-than- happy months were nearly over.

Sure enough, a few weeks later, I left not only Maple Cross behind but also my London experiences. I stayed in London for a few days. It was lonely. There were no kids anywhere to be seen. They were all evacuated. Once again, off I went into the unknown with my dolly, suitcase, gas mask and a note pinned to my coat with my name and destination written on it. I was a parcel.

The train stopped at Crewe and a nice soldier bought me an ice cream cone. What were cousins Hilda and Mildred like? I didn't know how old they were. Why wasn't I going to stay with Grandma Mendi who lived twenty miles from Stockport? So many questions with no answers to them. Also, what were these men in the black car up to? I wondered if a sixpence was offered to any other child. The train stopped and I had reached my destination. I knew I had arrived because the porters were yelling "Stockport, Stockport" and blowing on whistles.

There were no signs giving directions to towns and villages. They were removed in case we were invaded by the Germans. I was helped off the train with my belongings. There they were, waiting for me, Auntie Molly and Grandma Leah. I was relieved that they were smiling and running towards me with open arms. Kissy, kissy and hugs. This was new to me.

First we walked two miles to Grandma's house. Granddad Leah was sitting there waiting. He was a large man with a big leather belt around his waist. He also grew a huge white moustache which drooped over his mouth. When he kissed me, it was wet and I shuddered at the feel of it. After eating, Auntie Molly walked me to her house three miles away. I was so tired. Waiting for us were my cousins – Hilda, 10 years old and Mildred, four years old. I shared a bed with them. Auntie Molly put Mildred in the middle. She got squeezed in and she didn't like it. Hilda and I walked and giggled until a warning was shouted to shut up or else. I wasn't upset at the thought of sleeping with them.

Grandma and Grand Dad Leah

Auntie Molly and Uncle Arthur liked me. Once again, I settled into the routine with another family. Auntie Molly and Uncle Arthur were very nice to me. Uncle Arthur had a sense of humor which made me smile.

I really enjoyed the school. It was built in a square with a grass green in the centre. My teacher was Miss Graham whom I really liked. She made me "milk monitor" which made me feel important. My responsibility was to find out the number in each class that day and then leave that amount of bottles of milk at their door. Any milk that was left I could drink. I've enjoyed milk ever since. I think it gave me strong bones.

I did receive a little more attention because I was an evacuee. Hilda was in the same class as me and I began to feel she didn't like me. She was jealous and must have felt threatened. Also Mildred, her younger sister, was a "Shirley Temple" cutie with blonde curly hair. She was everybody's favorite. Even I wanted some of the attention she received.

Hilda would do naughty things and blame me. I remember when she put her fingers into a chip pan of solid fat then telling Auntie Molly it was me.

Another time she found a baby bird and fed it in a makeshift box. I wanted to give it a worm, so I did. The next day it died and she told everyone I killed it. Then we started to fight after she said things (whatever "things" means) about me.

At this time the adults were aware of what was going on. Then one day I was told I was going to live with Grandma and Granddad Leah. All I could think of was Granddad's big belt and wet mustache. Because I was between 10 and 11, I was allowed to finish my school year at the same school. But I was moved straight away to Grandma's carrying, guess what, my gas mask, case and dolly.

The four months I walked from Grandma's to the same school. It was a long way. Also I had to pass a group of boys going in the opposite way to their school. They would gang up on me and push me around. I was scared and I told Miss Graham. The headmaster, Mr. Duke, gave me a note to take to Cale Green School where the boys went. Their headmaster asked me to point the boys out, which I did. They didn't bother me again.

To my shame I learnt something from this experience. I would pass a little girl when I was on my way to school. Out of the blue I stopped her, my feet planted apart, and said to her, "Show me your knickers. Go on, show me your knickers." She would look up to me with frightened eyes and pull her dress up to show me the bottom of her knickers. "OK," I would say, laugh, and pass on. I did this for several days. This particular day she just looked at me and smiled. As I repeated my command, I noticed she was looking over my shoulder. I turned around and I cringed … there stood her big sister, who must have been fifteen. The warning … what she would do to me if it happened again. The power of intimidation that I learnt from the Cale Green boys didn't last long. I never tried that stunt again. Coward that I was.

By Christmas 1940, I had become familiar with Grandma's house; a terraced one with three bedrooms upstairs plus a bathroom. The toilet, which was a flush one, was outside the house. Downstairs was the parlor which was hardly used. The living room was used all the time, and the scullery for cooking and laundry. Then there was the dreaded cellar where the coat was kept. It had a stone floor and was very cold and damp. I began to hate it.

The bombing had just started on the Manchester and Liverpool docks. The cellar was where we went until the "all clear" sounded. Grandma Leah and Auntie Phyllis (my mother's unmarried sister) would sit on wooden chairs and I slept on a ladder placed between two chairs. I had to lie with my arms by my side. I thought I was in a coffin. I was totally unaware, as the bombs dropped, that death lurked around the corner.

There were times I was tired when I went to school. Stockport was a target as it had a viaduct that was joined by train to Manchester. Grandma was a dear, but I had reservations about Granddad with that belt of his, and he never smiled. Everything was so serious. I never laughed much in that house.

Looking back, they had such a responsibility with a ten-year-old on their hands. They were both very Victorian and very regimental. Bed by nine. Bath on Friday with ears cleaned, hair washed, and a laxative. Breakfast was at eight and it was always porridge. Sunday we had meat, veg. and potatoes followed by a pudding of some sort.

Monday, bubble and squeak, which was Sunday's leftovers fried up
... ugh! Tuesday, sausage and mash. Wednesday, beans and chips.
Thursday, meat pie. Friday, fish and Saturday, whatever there was.
Week in, week out ... it never changed. Grandma's treat was sugar
on bread called a "sugar butty."

Grandma was always knitting. I learned to knit by watching her
hour after hour. Granddad, who had retired, was called back to work
as a signalman on the railroad. He worked the 11pm to 7 am shift.
When I came down for breakfast he was always sitting on his stool
eating his breakfast. The one thing I noticed ... he sometimes had
an egg or a tomato. I would watch him peel them with such finesse.
I never had one and I wondered why? Not aware at my age they were
scarce during the war. I also hated seeing him sitting there not saying
anything, but I knew he could see me.

Because of the toilet being outside, I had a chamber pot under the
bed. It was my responsibility to empty it before I went to school.
This particular morning there was no way I was going to walk past
Granddad carrying this smelly thing, so I opened my bedroom window and threw the contents out. That made me feel good!

The new school I attended was Co-Ed but with a difference. The
boys and girls were in separate classrooms. I liked this school and
excelled in my studies, becoming top of the class. At the same time,
my interests were swimming and tap dancing lessons, which my
father paid for. I swam at the local bath but, unknown to Grandma, I
would go and swim at a large open-air pool because it had several
diving boards. Until someone yelled at me, "Wait till your Grandma
hears of you diving off the top board." I was back at the local pool
fast.

To me, everything seemed to happen without warning. When
Hilda visited Grandma's we would be friends. On this visit we went
off to the park to play. That kept us busy for a while then, what else
can we do? "I know," said I, observing a policeman's call in the station box. "You open the door, Hilda, and I'll yell fire at Didsbury
Road." I yelled into the box as loud as I could.

I was giggling as I turned to see Hilda bolting down the street.
Then a person was standing in front of me and I found I was staring
at a large silver button. Slowly looking up, there he was ... the severe

face of a large policeman. Putting his hands on my ten-year-old shoulder, he growled, "Well, well, and who have we here?!" Dropping his hands, he then pulled out a pencil and notebook. "Name," he said. My eyes were transfixed on him as I quavered. "Jean Davis, sir." Without any change of voice, he said, "Address." "96 Dale Street, sir." I gulped – in a rush, I quite gratuitously added, "and my cousin's name is Hilda Bower and she lives in Adwood. She was with me." He dismissed me with, "Your parents will hear about this." Whew!   What an escape, I said to myself, he's not going to tell my parents, they're in London. Wait till I see you, Hilda, running off like that. As I walked towards Grandma's, I started to rethink my situation. I'm not going back to Grandma's; maybe they know what I've done. Although I had never seen him use it, Granddad's black belt came to mind. Would he … ? Well, you never know.

I became worried so I went and sat in an above-ground air raid shelter which was near Grandma's, to hide. I sat there for what seemed hours. I knew it was late as it began to get dark. By then I was really scared to go home. My mind was filled with being stripped, going to prison, and worse than that, my parents finding out.

Suddenly a chill went over me as I heard, "Jean, Jean, where are you?" I kept hoping it would go away as I heard repeatedly, "Jean, Jean, where are you?" It was my Grandma's voice calling. Unable to stand it any longer, I ran out of the shelter towards the flashlight. Not a word was said until we reached home. "Get into the house," she snapped. I followed her into the house. To my horror, my mother was there. I stood petrified as Grandma said, "A policeman was here telling us what you and Hilda have been up to and that we would be receiving a letter." Then I was given a lecture on my behavior and sent to bed.

The next week a letter arrived informing us about this crime. We were to appear in the Judge's Chambers in Stockport. It was a well behaved Jean that week. I don't know about Hilda.

My mother being there was a coincidence. She, I was told, had come to stay with us. This was upsetting, especially finding out she was to sleep with me. My mother stayed around seven months. She was hired immediately as a bus conductor. I didn't see her too often but I was aware she had many near misses with the bombing when she worked the Stockport-to-Manchester shift.

She had a great companion in her sister, Auntie Phyllis. They were like peas in a pod. Off they would go, make-up and dressed to the nines, to a pub called The Charlston, which had a dance hall. I remember it was close to our Air Force Base in Winslow. The odd time Phyllis would bring an airman home.

I always knew when my mother had been out with Phyllis because when she climbed into bed she smelled of whisky or gin. I tried to sleep away from her because, to my disgust, she would wet the bed and it would touch me. I never said anything. At that time I never knew why she left London then returned to it months later. After my mother left, I was relieved.

Auntie Molly, Hilda, my mother and I went to the court house to be in front of the judge. After climbing many steps, we entered a huge building. My mother was directed to a marble, curved staircase and told the door number. Everything was big and very intimidating. I tried to catch Hilda's eye but she wouldn't look at me. We were told to wait outside a door.

Eventually the door opened and we were beckoned to go inside. There he sat, dressed in black, sitting behind a large desk. He had a round, red face and wooly hair. He crooked his hand which told us to come forward whilst saying, "Mothers, you stay where you are."

Then he addressed us: "Do you know why you are here?" We both nodded.

He proceeded, "Do you see this black book in front of me? What are your names?"

"Jean Davis and Hilda Bowe," we replied whilst holding back tears.

"I am writing your names in this book. They will remain in there forever for the crime you have committed."

I quickly turned my head to look at my mother and Auntie Molly, just in time to see them wipe a quick smile off their faces. I tried to figure that out. The judge continued, his deep voice boring into me.

"What did you shout into the emergency box?"

"Fire at Didsbury Road, sir," I croaked.

Leaning forward he continued, "What if an air raid was in progress and bombs were dropping somewhere else and the fire engines that YOU (pointing at us) had sent to Didsbury Road were needed somewhere else? People may have been injured or killed. Do you <u>understand</u> what I am saying?"

Both of us are like jelly as we tearfully replied, "Yes, sir, we're very sorry." At this point the tears flowed.

Looking over his glasses, he said, "I think they have learned their lesson, don't you, mothers? Take them away, they're dismissed."

All fears of going to prison left my mind. We were lectured on the way home about war being a serious thing.

Another time, playing with my cousin Alan next to a high wall with glass stuck on the top of it, I dared him to climb over the top of the wall to see what was on the other side. Alan, being a timid boy, refused. "Put your hands together, I'll put my foot in them, then push me upwards so we can see the other side."

He pushed me so hard I was able to pull myself up amongst the glass. Was I disappointed!   I was sure there were animals there but all there was were weeds and garbage. Disgusted, I jumped down to the ground and missed my timing, resulting in the glass ripping open my left hand.

Alan ran like a hare for Uncle Alf while I surveyed a badly torn hand. I cried all the way to the hospital where fifteen stitches were applied. Uncle Alf was very kind as I told him why it happened. Payment for being somewhere I shouldn't be.

Alan every now and then would come to Grandma's to play games with me. This day Grandma decided to leave us alone. "I'll be back in a while," she said. With a gleam in my eye, I said to Alan, "There's an old trunk in Grandma's bedroom; let's go and see what's inside it. We don't want to play games, do we?" Alan wasn't sure. I added, "There are lots of secrets in a trunk," I told him. "Alright," he said.

Grandma's bedroom was big and eerie looking. A huge bed with dark wooden chairs on either side. There was a wardrobe with a mirror in the centre. A fireplace that looked as if it had never been lit. The two windows were covered with white lace curtains. And there it was in the corner … the trunk. "This is the kind of trunk that pirates use," I said to Alan, who had a "we shouldn't be doing this" look on his face. "Come on, help me open it."

He pulled the latch back and we lifted the lid. I don't know what I expected to find, certainly not blankets and sheets. Slamming the lid shut, I picked up the cloth that had been on the trunk and neatly folded it, putting it back where it belonged. Then we investigated the wardrobe. Nothing in there but clothes.

"Look at that chair, Alan," I said. I had missed this funny-looking chair. We then took turns sitting on it. To my surprise the seat moved. I lifted it and wide eyed we saw underneath was a chamber pot. We laughed as we took turns once again sitting on the seat, but with a different thought in mind. We'd better get downstairs and start playing games till Grandma comes home.

Coming in from school the next day, Grandma was waiting with that "you're in trouble" look on her face. "What were you doing yesterday?" "Nothing," I said. "What were you and Alan doing in my bedroom, opening the trunk?" My mind was racing! How did she know we were in her bedroom? Also, how did she know we opened her trunk?

"How dare you go where you shouldn't," she said. Then she added the piece of the puzzle that was missing. "You folded the tablecloth on the trunk very neatly, Jean, instead of covering it over the trunk. Your nosiness found you out." Nothing was said after that.

Dear Alan. If Granddad was there, I would tickle Alan's knees under the table. He would look wide eyed trying to contain giggles. Granddad would look up and Alan's face would change to innocence. Like mine.

It was towards my last year in Stockport that I was faced with how other people perceived me. Jean Wood started calling me names with racial overtones. I couldn't understand her point. I had a fight with her. The next day she came over to me and said her mother had told her to apologize; it wasn't my fault my father was a black man. I was speechless with rage. All that name calling about my father, who was light coffee colored, wavy hair and handsome. My mind was beginning to open up.

Within the next few weeks I saw an ad in front of the local cinema. I was positive it was a movie my father was in and I went home to tell Grandma. Off we went to the cinema and, sure enough, there was my father's band on the screen. The movie was "The Ghost goes

West." I was so excited. I didn't tell anyone. They wouldn't have believed me. My father made two more movies after that.

It was before the government Eleven Plus exams that my father came to visit me. If you passed these exams it allowed you to continue on to a higher level of education. If not, you had to leave school at age fourteen. On this visit he informed me that I would be leaving Grandma Leah's and going to live in Haswell Plough with my Great-Grandma Mary, Grandma Mendi and Great-Great-Uncle George. I was not to tell Grandma Leah. I had to say I was going back to London. I have no idea why the lie. It may have been the bombing. This information, I believe, changed my life.

Knowing I wasn't staying in Stockport, I began to study less and less at school. The government exams became unimportant to me. At the Easter school exams, I dropped from top of the class to 19th. Even I was shocked! Needless to say, I failed the Eleven Plus. This should never have happened. The timing of my father was bad. Leaving Stockport sad. I would miss my cousins Alan and Eileen, also Grandma.

Once again the Stockport experience gave me lots to think about. I don't believe anyone missed me when I left. They may have been relieved!

Safe Once Again … or was I?

(Part I)

Leaving Grandma Leah's house
in July 1942.

With my suitcase, gas mask and my doll, I was once again on my way to another place of evacuation. This time to Haswell Plough, a hamlet in the County of Durham where my dad's mother, Grandma Mendi, lived with her mother, Great-Grandma Mary, and Great-Great-Uncle George.

My dad told me to tell Grandma Leah he was taking me to London to live with him and my mother. Why the lie, I don't know. Maybe it was not to hurt Grandma Leah's feelings. After all, I had been living with my mother's people from 1940 to 1942.

I knew Haswell Plough quite well. I had spent several summer holidays there and had made some friends. Grandma Mendi had just recently moved to Haswell Plough from Salford, Manchester, which was near Stockport. The German bombing had become very heavy. The Manchester Canal flowed past the end of Grandma Mendi's street. It was a prime target for air raids. Merchant ships landed with food and supplies from the U.S.A. and Canada; sailed into the Manchester docks.

Haswell Plough consisted of around two hundred council houses, which were rented to the coal miners at a reasonable price. "The Plough," as we called it, had a small grocery store, a pub and the miners' club. The work force was mostly in the coal mines where boys would leave school at fourteen to work in them. Because the need for coal was a main energy supply, the mines were running twenty-four hours a day with three eight-hour shifts.

Haswell Plough. Great Grandma Mary's House.

The miners in The Plough walked or rode their bikes to their shift, the nearest mine being four miles away. No pit baths and the pleasure of showers. The miners arrived home, coal black, and they bathed in galvanized tubs in hot water in front of the fire, the water being heated in kettles over an open fire grate. Katie Long, a next door neighbor, started two hours before George, her husband, arrived home, getting his tub ready. A daunting task.

The mines closed for a two-week holiday in the summer. Because of the war, all except one beach were barbed wired and mined, closing them down. Going to the greyhound races was enjoyed; also breeding pigeons.

Life for a miner was hard; also for the wife. Her treat, if you can call it that, was a visit to the miners' club on a Saturday night, enjoying sipping a glass of sherry or gin and tonic, the husband swallowing pints of beer and playing "Housie Housie" (Bingo).

Great-Great-Uncle George was my grandma's uncle. He had been retired for many years. He liked smoking his white clay pipe. When they broke he would send me to buy more for a penny-a-piece. I was fascinated, looking at him when he spoke in a strong Geordie accent and showing only two front teeth, which were as black as the coal, tobacco juice dripping from the side of his mouth. Great-Great-Uncle

George did make a shilling or two extra. He was a "knocker up." Using a long stick with a rubber end, he woke the early morning shift by knocking on the miners' bedroom windows to waken them.

Great-Grandma Mary was George's sister-in-law. It happened this way . . .

While living with Grandma Mendi from 1930 to 1937 in Salford, Manchester, she used to take me to visit Great-Grandma Mary in South Shields. Great-Grandma Mary was a widow. The three of us would then visit Great-Grandma Mary's brother-in-law, George Dale, and his wife, Kate. George was a younger brother of Joseph Dale, Great-Grandma Mary's dead husband.

George and Kate lived in a two-room stone cottage with stone floors. The cottages were built around 1820. Cooking was done over an open fireplace. Lifting on trivets, the cooking pans were moved over the fire. Fifteen cottages in a row. One tap and outhouse served these cottages. The floors were covered with handmade rag rugs. Two rooms in each cottage.

In 1936, Kate died and Mary, her sister-in-law, moved from South Shields to Haswell Plough to live and look after Great-Great-Uncle George. They never married.

Great-Grandma didn't talk to me very much but she did now and then put a penny in my hand to go and buy her Black Bullets, which were her favorite sweets. I would get one as a reward.

Here I am, surrounded by three adults born in the 1800s, and so Victorian. Although I was with Grandma Mendi until I was seven in 1937, I had only seen her six times since then. Such was my bonding with her when a small child. I became comfortable in this new/old environment very quickly. I lived in poverty but did not know it.

Grandma Mendi called me one day and told me I was to take her mother, Great-Grandma Mary, on a train journey to visit her nieces in Doncaster, Yorkshire. I was so nervous. I had only been in Haswell Plough three weeks and here I was, at eleven years old, with the responsibility of looking after Great-Grandma Mary on a long train journey. I followed everything my Grandma told me to do. My nerves were so bad I started wetting the bed again.

I took to school straight away, then the usual problem started when the kids saw my dad. The nick names ... "Lulu," "Queen of the Jungle," "FrizzyLiz" and "Fluffy Davis." "Fluffy" was the name that stuck.

I landed in a class appropriate for my age. It became obvious that I was above its curriculum and, much to my joy, I was put in the top class where I stayed until I left school at 14.

It is November 1942 and Great-Grandma is lying and dying on a small bed next to the fireplace. I watched my Grandma Mendi take care of her with such kindness and care. I was shown certain personal things to do to make Great-Grandma comfortable. My Grandma called her mum "Queenie." There were only 14 years between them. Grandma Mendi was born in Jarrow Workhouse for the Destitute in 1886. She was the product of a rape.

Christmas morning 1942 …

I wasn't feeling too well and so I lay on the couch under the window overlooking the street. Grandma, for a treat, poured out two glasses of home-made lemonade. I drank mine and when Grandma went into the scullery, I took a sip of hers. Not knowing I was being watched, Grandma came into the room and Great-Grandma raised herself from the bed and said: "She took some of your lemonade, Maggie." Grandma's fury was instant as she belted me one. I cried and lay down on the couch begging not to feel really poorly. I didn't want to be ill as my dad was coming to visit for two days and he was going to take me into Sunderland.

I felt a lot better on Boxing Day. The next day my dad took me into Sunderland and we had tea and little cakes in a cafe. I felt sick and went to the bathroom. Fear, fear! I am dying! I must be dying with all this blood. I spent four days terrified, knowing I was dying. I used old dust rags to help the flow then, thank goodness, the horror stopped. I convinced myself I wasn't going to die. On the way to school I threw the evidence into a field. The end of January, it happened again. I prayed I would be gone. Don't let this happen to me again. I hid the evidence with the intention of using the field.

Coming home from school that day, Kate Long, the next door neighbor, met me to tell me Great-Great-Grandma Mary had died and the bedroom was being cleaned and her body washed. I got into the house and quietly went upstairs hoping to do what I had to do, when the loud voice of Mrs. Lee said: "Good God, Maggie, these are not yours." I hastily retreated. The next morning, my Grandma told me to sit down, she wanted to talk about what had been found under the bed. I jumped up and as I ran out of the house, mortified, I yelled: "I know all about it. You don't have to tell me. (I knew nothing.) Grandma called after me: "Well, that's that, Miss Know-it-all." Never a word was said after that. What did appear on the bed was a handmade belt with two strings front and back, and a package of "Kotex" for me. It was a slow journey being educated. Listening to girls at school, I put the pieces together. This will happen forever. I wished I was dead.

Great-Grandma Mary was buried and the bedroom returned to normal. There were extra coupons supplied for the food that was bought for this occasion. It seemed odd to me that the adults were laughing and filling their mouths with all kinds of cakes. We had just put Great-Grandma down a hole in the ground with Grandma Mendi whispering: "Goodbye, Queenie."

Safe Once Again ... or was I?

(Part II)

Great-Grandma's death returned us to normal. No more bedpans to flush down the outside toilet. No more washing her down. No more eyes watching, and no more creeping about to avoid making a noise. Her single bed, which was placed four feet from the open fire, our only means to cook, was on its way upstairs to Grandma's bed-room for me to sleep on. It was replaced with a grey lumpy settee used by Great- Great-Uncle George, who sat there sucking on his clay pipe.

It didn't stay normal for long.

About a month later, in the middle of the night, there was loud knocking on the door. Great-Great-Uncle George didn't hear it. He was as deaf as a lamp post. Grandma and I went downstairs fearfully and stood looking at the door. We jumped as the knocking started again. Then came a voice. "Aunt Maggie it's me, Laurence, home from India." Grandma opened the door and there stood two soldiers in their uniforms with kit bags. Laurence (Great-Great-Uncle George's son) had brought with him George Stevenson, a friend in the army. He was very handsome.

Soldier George.

Laurence and his friend, Georgy Stevenson, had been in India for four years. I remembered them from the old stone two-room cottages.

They were sent back to England to fight the war elsewhere. They were on one month's leave and then they reported to London for further instructions. The two slept with Great-Great- Uncle George.

I was fascinated by them, especially Georgy, because I remember the kiss on the cheek he gave me at the old cottage when he thought I was asleep. A circus and fair were in the village for a few days and everyone went. I happened to see Laurence with Cilla Hull, a local girl. When Laurence became aware that I was following them he turned, gave me a shilling, and told me to "buzz off." I disappeared fast.

I followed him because he was with Cilla. Everyone knew Cilla, who was eighteen and man crazy. One night at the church hall dance, a few of us were in the cloakroom giggling like little kids and in came Cilla, her face painted, and looking at us with scorn. To our horror, she bent down and took her knickers off, put them in her handbag, picked up her coat and laughed as she left. We stood there not saying a word. I went back into the dance saying to myself: "Why did she take her knickers off and why did she leave the dance halfway through?"

The month went by quickly and life returned to normal. I had begun to talk to a boy up the street who went to grammar school. His name was Keith. I met him at the soda shop. He was drinking lemonade. He was very nice. He said: "Sorry I can't buy you a lemonade. I'm financially embarrassed." I didn't know what that meant but it sounded so important. Wasn't he wonderful? He was "financially embarrassed." Now and again he would stop in front of the gate whilst walking his greyhound dog. I would peek through the curtains and wave. One day my Grandma said: "Wish he wouldn't stop in front of our gate. His dog leaves a dollop every time." I smiled, knowingly.

The dances were what I looked forward to. The band consisted of a violin, piano and drums. All amateur musicians. The sound was awful but the beat was good. I was never directly asked to dance by a male but waited patiently for the three barn dances where we re-volved in a circle; men in the middle and women on the outside. When the music stopped, you danced with the man/boy opposite you. This was what taught us to dance the various rhythms. In the meantime, I danced with Nellie who could lead very well. Sometimes the vicar popped his head in to see if things were OK.

There were other dances in surrounding villages which we did attend but it was always four or more miles to walk home in the pitch black. The last bus left before the dance finished. I couldn't miss a dance.

Grandma started up her didlehum clubs again. She had become aware that many miners had no money at holiday time and Christmas. She put a system together, where they bought an envelope for sixpence, and each payday they came and put in a set amount for that envelope. Anything over sixpence a receipt was given. Payment came the week before the holidays and at Christmastime. The procedure could be stopped at any time but the money was frozen until payout. Not everyone contributed. Many a smile and "Thank you, Maggie" came from the ones who did. I helped counting and filling the envelopes. Grandma was frugal and her take on money was if you wanted something you saved the double amount of what it cost, then you bought it. Every so often I would see her slip a coin or two into a green tea caddy with a huge dragon painted on it. "That's for a rainy day" was her explanation.

One of those "rainy days" came as a trip to the city of Sunderland, a long bus ride away, to see a film called "Gone With The Wind." Before we entered the cinema, she said to me: "Take note of what you are watching." I was amazed by the film but also shocked at the way black men and women were treated. Years later, I realized Grandma's "take note" was some sort of lesson to be learned.

I became very aware that the traveling salesmen, Martin Dodds, stopped at Grandma's house for his lunch every month. Out came a tablecloth which covered the usual linoleum. Two matching tea cups and saucers with one plate were carefully placed. Most noticeable was ... out came from her hair the metal curlers and off came the pinny (apron) that covered Grandma's dress. This was royalty arriving, and my Grandma's house was chosen to be host.

On one particular visit I had a terrible headache. I watched Martin Dodds gently unwrap his sandwich and carefully place it on the plate. Grandma of course supplied the biscuit. I heard her mentioning my headache. To my dismay, he stopped everything, motioned me to sit on a chair. He then proceeded to stroke the side of my head with the tips of his fingers, murmuring something at the same time. After a few minutes he stopped and said: "There, that should do it. It has gone now, hasn't it?"

I didn't have the nerve to say anything but "yes." Smiling, he sat down, picked up his sandwich whilst Grandma looked at him as if he was Jesus Christ himself. This one day a month was important to Grandma. She was a somebody As I write these vignettes down, it reinforces in my mind what a most unusual human being Grandma was. I was learning from her all the time.

Take the time when we bussed to the nearest village to buy her a new corset. We had few clothing coupons and we had to spend them wisely. As soon as I entered the cooperation store, I saw it. I knew it was for me. The low neck, pinched-in waist and brilliant red. I rushed over and touched it, my eyes seeing a vision of me as I wore it to the Saturday church dance. Everyone would be looking at me. Only a thirteen - year-old could think this way. Then reality set in as the "oohs" turned to groans. My clothing coupons for the year were used up. Walking over to Grandma, saying many times- "There's a lovely red dress over there" and "You should see it" adding long sighs. Grandma grumbled all the way out of the store followed by me with a bag and a red dress, me smiling, oblivious at that time of the sacrifice she had made for me. No corset.

A bunch of us kids led by an older girl put on a concert to make money towards buying a "spitfire" plane - our contribution towards the war effort - telling Grandma that we had to make as much money as we could. The tickets were one shilling. My contribution was to sing and dance. I managed to sell five tickets. When I asked Grandma for her shilling she said: "I'm going to give you one week s pension. I swallowed, as one week's pension was 10 shillings. That was her total income besides what my dad paid her for my keep. I loved her to pieces.

The next day, going downstairs, I heard her and a neighbor talking about the concert in glowing terms. Then my Grandma said: "Well, something has to be done about her tits. They were jiggling up and down like a yo-yo." I back tracked up the stairs, my face red. I could have killed her. That was my Grandma.

Once in a while off we would travel to South Shields to visit an elderly man named Ned Liddle. She, as she told me, had gone to school with him. I wasn't comfortable visiting Ned. He was a gentle soul who coughed all the time. As Grandma explained, Ned had been wounded in the first world war and suffered from mustard poison gas. His two rooms were sparse. One room had a bed, a chair and an old cupboard for his few clothes. The other had a table, two chairs, a cold water cracked sink in the corner, a cupboard for his meagre rations, various hooks in the wall, and the odd rag mat on the floor. When we stayed overnight, Ned would sleep in a chair whilst we slept in his bed. I never told Grandma but I'm sure she knew there were fleas in his bed. Such a difference from where we lived. The furniture may have been worn and very old fashioned but it was meticulously clean. Ned would come and visit us and he would sleep with Great-Great-Uncle George.

Two things happened the weekend Grandma visited Ned on her own. One was my going to the pictures to see Dianna Durbin. I was told to come straight home after the first showing. In those days, you could go into the pictures anytime. If it was halfway through, then you stayed to see the rest at the second showing. Grandma's away, the mouse will play. The picture was wonderful and so I stayed for the second showing. By the time I arrived home at 12 o'clock at night, all I could hear in my thirteen-year-old ears was Great-Great-Uncle George yelling: "This is no time to come home. Wait till I tell your Grandma. She will give you a licking." Grandma came home. Not a word was said. But the whole of The Plough knew I came home late.

The second incident was a great time to look in the wardrobe drawers. Nothing of great interest, until I pulled out an envelope. I was about to shove it back but decided to open it. I found myself looking at a photo of a little boy with dark curly hair. I stared at it with curiosity wondering who he was. Turning it over I read: "Love from your grandson, Derek." My thoughts flitted here and there from ... "It can't be Grandma's grandson" to "If he was, how can this be?" For some reason, I felt threatened. When she arrived home, I told her straight out that I been nosy and looked in her wardrobe drawer and found this photo. She was evasive, saying it was someone she knew.

Also, my dad was visiting next week and he would tell me.

I spent the week confused and angry. What was behind it? I know now it was no coincidence that my dad was coming. She had sent for him. He arrived ten days later. After supper, he said he wanted to talk to me. It went like this. He, my dad, said . . .

Derek was indeed my dad's son and a lady named May was his mother. She, May, was a nice lady and the sad thing was that she wasn't my mother. Although I had a child's version of my mother, I didn't like him saying that. I don't know why. Then he went on to say that May and Derek lived in London and that the bombing had been terrible. Would I mind if they came up to The Plough for a month's rest? I said it was fine with me. What else could I answer to a question like that? The conversation was ended and my only input was "it was fine with me."

My innocence glowed around me. I knew nothing about adult sexuality, or how babies came about. My mind was still frozen in time. Was I found in a cabbage on the doorstep or did I come from my mother's belly? The latter was definitely not true. Also, what was this May doing in my dad's life? After all, where was Elsie? Around July, Grandma informed me May and Derek were to arrive the next day. I was to meet them at Durham Station. By this time, I was hostile towards them coming; also jealous of this other grandchild.

I didn't trust my Grandma as much. She had secrets. When the train stopped and passengers came off, my eyes searched for May and Derek. I was not going to smile; I was going to be as unfriendly as possible. Then, there they were. Nothing like I expected. May, a blonde, fair skin lady dressed to the nines. Derek was the most beautiful little four-year-old boy. He put his hand in mine straight away and smiled. I was lost. Before we ever got on the bus to The Plough, I had already spent my precious sweetie coupons on a bar of chocolate for him. He was a lovely child. May had a Cockney accent but she looked like a film star.

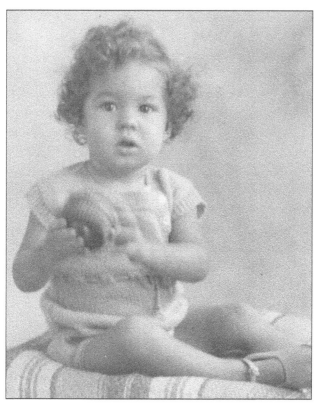

Baby Derek.

It was the summer holidays and I had lots of time to spend with Derek. I took him to the pictures and on long walks in the country to see cows and sheep for the first time.

Taking sandwiches on a picnic with other kids and eating them before we arrived at the picnic spot, which was a huge haystack built like a house, we would sit propped up against it and look down at The Plough nestled peacefully between farmland. Derek's big joy was blackberry picking. Off we would go with our Billy cans, his delight at every one he picked. One for the can and one in his mouth. One day, the cans were full so I took off my vest and used it. I told him never to tell Grandma. So he helped me hide the stained vest in a small windowsill in the outside toilet.

I tried to be on my best behavior with May, but now and again I snapped back. She told Grandma, who warned me not to be rude to her. May came with me to the dance at a nearby village. On the bus home, there was a lot of noise from two soldiers who were drunk. The conductress stopped the bus and ordered them off. They refused, and a skirmish started. The police came and, after a fight, took them away. May and I were called as witnesses. We were in the courthouse ready to be called when the two soldiers stood up, jumped on several tables and crashed through the windows. Glass, blood, everywhere! The court was dismissed and we never knew what the ending was.

May and Derek came and went. Life continued. George Stevenson married.

It was about this time I heard Grandma exclaiming: "George Stevenson is marrying Peggy Donahue! He must be crazy. Too soon after four years in India." I was mortified. I had developed a crush on George. That week Peggy asked me to be her bridesmaid. The evening before the simple wedding in Chapel, a knock came at the door and George came to see Grandma. What about I don't know. All I know, at the back door he pulled me to him and gave me a long kiss. At thirteen, I was thrilled to pieces. Within six months, he left Peggy and never returned.

It was still summer when I was informed that my parents were coming for a visit. I hadn't seen my mother, Elsie, since I lived in Stockport two years ago. The churning in my stomach started again.

They arrived on a Friday. The exchange between us was fine. I just sat and listened to them talking with Grandma. My parents decided that the three of us would go to the beach the next day. Off we went on the bus to the one beach that was open. My bathing suit was a blue woolie one made before the war. UGH! The day was pleasant and chatty.

After supper at Grandma's, I went to the pictures and my parents went to the miner s club. My dad took his guitar and, like the last time he came, he entertained those who were there. I came out of the pictures around nine o'clock. I still had a two-mile walk home. As I rounded the comer to my street, Kate Long was running towards me. On reaching me, she said: "Don't go into Grandma's, come into my house, there's been a fight between your parents." My heart sank. "God, she's here again" I murmured through gritted teeth. No way was I going into Kate's house. I walked into Grandma's and there she was sitting on the lumpy couch, tears on her face. What a mess. I gave her the same look that I gave her when, at seven years old, she slapped me. Then I walked out.

Kate told me that some woman in the miners' club had told my mother about May and Derek being here. She went berserk and violent. On arriving back at Grandma's, she took scissors and slashed my dad's clothes up. My parents were gone the next day, leaving me with fear and bewilderment. No further explanation was given, except my Grandma said to me: "Jean remember, no matter what your mother does, she is your mother." What had occurred just embarrassed me. I knew nothing at all about how babies came about and human sexuality. The implication of this situation went over my head. All I thought was: "She had to come and spoil everything." But what has always stayed with me … "No matter what your mother does, she is your mother."

I began to weigh it up carefully, over and over again, what my father had said. May was a nice lady and the sad thing was that she wasn't my mother. A few days later, a lovely white swimsuit arrived in the mail from my parents. I guess the blue woolie one didn't go over so well.

We were now into late September and allowed off school to pick potatoes. We went from farm to farm. It was hard work but so much fun. We were paid sixpence a day. We took our own bucket which we were allowed to take home full. The Foster Farm was my favorite because we worked with Italian prisoners-of-war. The one song seemed to be their favorite: "Amapola, My Pretty Little Poppy" they sang in Italian.

Working with one of them was fun. He would laugh and show me a picture of someone in his family. Also, they were given lunch in a bag and often they would give us a biscuit. We squirted milk right from the cow into our mouths. Coming home one day with a bunch from school, I was dying to pee. What was I going to do? We were still a couple of miles from The Plough. I wet my pants. I could see a small rill (stream) ahead and I yelled to the others: "Bet you can't jump the rill." Some of them tried and crossed it; so did I, except I didn't quite make it. Splash! What a relief. An ingenious way to solve a problem.

It is now Christmas 1943.

I opened a cupboard by mistake and found a round, brown plastic handbag with a bright white strap. Grandma had had it made by the lady up the street for my Christmas present. Damn it! I kept quiet. On Christmas morning, I knew she was happy when I showed surprise and such joy at her gift. My dad sent me one pound which I put in the new handbag.

Christmas night I went with Nellie, my girlfriend, to the village of Thomly to see the film "Holiday Inn." Thornly was a four-mile walk to The Plough, mostly on a country road. We started off after the film finished to go home. Because of the war, everywhere was black. We did have our small flashlight, which was not much use. The sky was dark with the moon peeking out now and again. We had walked about half a mile when I screamed: "I've lost my handbag!" I was crying and saying: "We will never find it." Nellie and I turned around and took little steps back towards the picture house. "Please, God, please God, let me find my handbag." With no exaggeration, the moon popped out and I yelled: "There it is, something white, there!" I bent down and it was the straps of my handbag. "Oh, thank you, God!" I said, over and over.

Best friend Nellie.

Around May '44, Grandma said I was to go to London for the day, catching a train the night before and returning on the 8 pm train the next day. I was to be met by my mother. What a whirlwind it proved to be. First we visited a small room where she said she lived. The room had a single bed, chair, wardrobe and small table. What is she doing here? I wondered. I was introduced to a serious looking lady as, "This is my daughter, Jean" full stop. Then we went off on a shopping spree.

My mother had the coupons. We went into every shop in Oxford Street. We finally chose from meager pickings a grey skirt and jacket and a pale blue blouse. The blouse fastened with tiny bows, no buttons. Off came my gym slip and blouse which were placed in a bag. Then we had dinner at Lyon's Corner House, Marble Arch. My sandals, which still squeaked, had to be replaced. Off we went looking for shoes. Finally a navy blue pair were chosen which had a heel. I could hardly walk in them. Into the bag went the sandals.

Now we went to meet her man-friend at Oxford Circus Tube. Before I got to meet him, I tripped getting on to the train and the right heel of my shoe fell off. As I looked, there was one big nail holding the heel to the shoe. As soon as my mother's friend saw my plight, off we went here and there to find a cobbler who fixed it, saying to my mother: "It's war time, luv. Ya lucky to have one nail in there."

Off we went again and I was introduced. I couldn't remember his name or what he looked like, only he seemed nice. Arriving at King's Cross for the train to Durham, the station was bedlam; troops all over the place. It quite unnerved me. They managed to get me a seat between a couple of soldiers and told me Durham was past York. Putting my bag with my gym slip and sandals on the rack above, I settled down clutching my handbag.

Within a short time the train was full. The corridors were tightly packed with troops standing, swaying back and forth as the train chugged on. It wasn't long before I realized most of the journey would be in the dark. No lights anywhere except for the odd match to light a cigarette. There I was in a compartment with nine men in the pitch black. It was surreal. There were one or two comments that went on here and there which meant nothing to me. All I could think was that Durham was the next stop after York.

The boy/man on my left side asked me my name and where I was going. I told him I had visited London for the day. Sitting there my mind was flitting all over the place but certainly not in this area. The boy/man suddenly kissed me, my face turned towards him, as he kissed me on the lips. I froze. What did I do? This happened again, but this time I kissed him back. No more, when the train started to slow down and porters' voices rang out: "York, York." One more kiss and he was gone. I never knew what he looked like. He never knew he had kissed a thirteen-year-old. Was he lonely? Did he survive the war and did he wonder what I looked like? My body was playing havoc with my mind.

I made a big mistake. I told a girl at school about the soldier on the train. Before I knew what happened, rumor got around that I nearly went off with a soldier but changed my mind. I had better tell my Grandma before someone else did. She listened with understanding, no recriminations. The next thing that happened embarrassed me, but I got over it. In the Northern Echo Newspaper the next week was written: (words to this effect)

"Any slander or gossip referring to my granddaughter, Jean Davis, will be addressed by Solicitors' name.

Margaret Mendi."

Until now … end of story.

Time was marching on and I knew that I had to leave school. I dreaded it. I loved school and the teachers. Also, I was a good student. My Grandma had already told me I would be going back to London to be with my parents. The idea of London sounded exciting to me. With my parents … that filled me with fear of the unknown. How could I live with my parents? Did Grandma know she, my mother, lived in this small room? Nobody told me anything. I was afraid to ask. I don't want to leave my Grandma, but I can't stay in The Plough. All there was was a pub, a shop and a miner's club.

My hormones were beginning to show. I had fallen madly in love with a boy I met at Easington Village. He said he liked me and it was a shame that I was going to London. The next day, which was a Saturday, I spent ages burning a sixpence in half. I was going to give half to him, telling him not to forget me. I held onto the two halves until the week I left for London. We only saw each other at the dance. How safe we were. Aunties, uncles, grandmas, you name it, would be at the dance. The time he walked me home was when he kissed me. I will love him forever. Now, what was his name?!!

Growing up wasn't easy … enduring the pain of a clothes peg pinched on my top lip to produce a cupid's bow like the film stars; heating the poker in the fire then wrapping around a lock of hair to make a curl. One morning the poker was too hot and it burnt through the hair creating a dreadful smell. I can still hear Grandma's voice: "What's that smell down there?" I pulled another piece of hair over the bald spot. I would buy red sweeties for lipstick and use gravy browning on my legs for stockings Dogs in the neighborhood were sniffing around me. That was the extent of the adult world for me.

Going back to London after five years evacuation held a certain kind of excitement, but staying with my parents created anxiety and fear. What do I do? I don't know them. How do I behave? I'm still wearing a gym slip. Never heard of a bra. I still wear woolie vests to keep me warm and children's knickers. I don't want to leave school but I have to. Saying goodbye to The Plough and Grandma was painful, yet I knew the excitement of what was ahead.

Thank God I didn't know what was ahead! I left July 30th. - one month before I was 14 on August 22nd.

1944-1952

London

War still on until 1945

It was August 1944 and here I was, after five long years of evacuation to various places, finding my way on the train traveling from my Grandma's in Haswell to London to live with two parents I hardly knew, only having lived with them from age seven to nine. At the age of fourteen I still wore my school gym slip and carried my doll, Margaret, gas mask and suitcase which my Grandma had packed for me. Her peck on the cheek and "Don't forget … whatever your mother does, remember she is still your mother," whatever that meant, was embedded in my memory.

I can't really believe I am returning to London after five years to live with them. The vivid incidents that happened after they visited me during the past two years had left me worried, uneasy and very confused. I fretted between the excitement of the unknown and holding back tears of the future all the way from Haswell Plough to King's Cross Station, London.

What was this May and Derek to do with me? How come this woman should have been my mother? I know it had something to do with the last visit my parents made to The Plough. I was almost home and Katie, my next door neighbor, came rushing towards me, yelling: "Get into my house, Jean, your parents have had a terrible fight." My first thoughts … it had to be something she's done. No way was I going to Katie's house.

I walked into Grandma's and there she was (my mother) sitting on the sofa crying. I remember giving her a dirty look. I couldn't understand what the row was all about. Nobody explained to me my mother's position. The fracas was caused as a neighbor explained … someone at the miner's club had told my mother that May and Derek had visited. Is that why my mother cut my father's clothes up? It didn't seem much of a reason to go crazy about. I was so innocent, knowing nothing about adults involvement with each other. I just couldn't figure it out.

Arriving at King's Cross I put my things together and scrambled off the train. To my relief, there was my father waiting at the end of the platform. I managed a weak "Hello." He stared at me for a moment then said: "Don't I get a kiss?" I was so embarrassed. To kiss a man in front of all these people. I looked both ways to see if anyone was watching. I dutifully pecked him on the cheek. We walked out of the station to where or what. For the first time, I felt silly carrying my dolly.

My dad explained to me on the long walk from the station to where we lived – a basement flat next to Gasfield Street – that we had lived there before the war. I felt comfortable with that as I remembered the area and the name of the shops. My dad did all the talking. He never enquired about my journey, school or Grandma. He went on to explain that my mother would not be at the flat for another four weeks. She had just had a hysterectomy (whatever that was) and she would be going to the countryside for convalescence, but we would be visiting her the next day.

My mother was an enigma. Not many pleasant memories reminded me of her. Suddenly it seemed we were at the flat. I knew the address – 92 Great Titchield Street, W.1. – because I had written one or two letters there. It was a five-story building and, like all the buildings I had seen so far, it was dirty. The five years of war with the bombing, and now the rockets, contributed to that. Everything looked grimy and broken. Bomb damage was everywhere.

The flats had five steps going up to a main door. My dad pointed down through some railings to a large yard. On the right side were two large, filthy windows with brown strips of paper glued to them. (The war was still on and this was protection from flying glass.) The windows were opposite a wall with an opening that went under the pavement where we stood looking down. Underneath us were coal cellars, except they were empty. There was little coal to be had owing to the war.

Climbing up the five steps to the main entrance we turned left and walked down ten dirty steps into a large filthy area. On both sides of this area were two doors leading to the three-roomed flats. My dad pointed to the right where, upon opening the door, I found we were in a bedroom. To the left was the kitchen overlooking dustbins and dirt. To the right was the living room overlooking the coat cellars underneath the pavement up above.

The place reeked of dampness and cold. The kitchen consisted of a galvanized sink with a cold water tap, a small wooden table with two uncomfortable chairs, a home-made cupboard with dishes in it and a gas stove placed next to an old iron cooker/fireplace inserted into the wall. This ancient cooker hadn't been used in years.

The bedroom was furnished with a bed, a chest of drawers and a wardrobe. The far right room had a lighter look about it and yet, to my dismay, it was furnished with the same furniture I remembered from 1939! I remembered sleeping on that bed-settee and hiding under the bedclothes because I was frightened. A shudder went through me. Then I heard my dad say: "You'll be sleeping on this bed-settee." "No, no" I could hear my brain saying. Was it only yesterday I was in quiet Haswell Plough, surrounded by fields? The excitement of London was vanishing quickly. I don't want to be here! I don't want to be with these parents!

This transition from Grandma's was traumatic. I was afraid. Instead of waking up in Grandma's soft bed, I woke up on that hard sofa, cold because there wasn't any coal; cold water to wash myself. Certainly no porridge, just bread and jam.

The toilet outside had not been washed in months. Not even newspaper to clean oneself. UGH! I sat alone all morning. Dad fried sliced potatoes dipped in butter for lunch, then we visited mother in the afternoon.

On entering the ward I did what I was supposed to do … smile and say hello. She looked presentable; hair and make-up just right. I felt weird. I didn't know what to talk about. The conversation was awkward. She helped by discussing her operation, finishing off, to my discomfort, by lifting her gown and revealing a huge, heavily stitched stomach. I clenched my teeth and held my breath. I was glad when the visit was over.

Returning to the flat, I chatted non-stop telling my dad about the last month at school. I had finished top of the class. Also, the big thing was that on the last day of school we finished off playing rounders. I hit the ball clean over the school wall and the team I was on won. I didn't want to leave school but had no choice. I had failed the beastly "11 Plus" exam. My chance of a further education was stopped at age 11.

The girls who left school at fourteen either looked for domestic work in wealthy homes, sought work in the city or stayed home to help mum. Most of the boys finished off as miners shoveling coal, a terrible occupation. In The Plough, I often gazed out of my bedroom window to look at an old mine shaft on the hill at the back of the garden. This mine had collapsed in the late 1900s. Ninety-two miners were killed. The bodies were never recovered and the mine closed forever. My friend, Nellie, sent me a commemorative mug of the one hundred year anniversary. I still have it.

Here I was, one day back in London, fourteen-years-old, no work, and worried about what's going to happen to me. I had the impression my dad was not much interested in my chatter as he interrupted, telling me about his work. He said he played in a Rhumba Band at two dinner nightclubs just off Piccadilly Circus, one named "The Princess," the other "The Potomac." They were situated on two streets back to back and joined by an underground tunnel where the kitchen served both clubs. There was also a swing band. Both bands played on a revolving stage where they exchanged positions twice during the night; as one band disappeared, the other appeared.

My dad went on to tell me that he leaves the flat around 6:30pm and arrives home about midnight, and I would be alone whilst my mother was in hospital. "Alone," I said to myself … alone in this dark, damp, underground flat. I looked straight ahead, not saying a word. My stomach was tight.

By the time we reached the flat, he told me he would take me to the clubs the first two night home. That perked my interest but not for long. I never wanted to be in London. I wanted to go back to The Plough. What was going to happen to me? All I could think of was me.

The first club I visited was "The Potamac." I was told to sit at a table in the corner of the room and then, when the bands changed places, I would go with my dad's band through the tunnel into "The Princess Club." It sounded exciting. Sitting in my school gym slip taking all this in, I was thrilled to see people coming in; women dressed in beautiful gowns with jewelry around their necks or in their ears; some of the men wearing tuxedos or evening jackets. It was unreal. I thought I was in a movie. I was so engrossed I failed to hear a waiter say: "What would madam like to order?" I looked at him and he repeated, "What would madam like to order?" He had a twinkle in his eyes. I felt so important. My friends at school would never believe this! Looking at him, I whispered, "Could I have sausage and mash, please?" He smiled and bowed, then left. I didn't get my sausage and mash but what he brought me looked nice, so I ate it. It tasted good. Walking home later, my dad told me that my order of sausage and mash had caused much laughter in the kitchen.

The clubs were decorated with different sized tables placed around a small dance floor. At the sides of the room were alcoves. Each club had a different decor. Two things thrilled me. One was rushing with the band underground, so that they could play in the other club, and trying to avoid the staff working in the kitchen. The other was my dad dressed in a colorful Rhumba outfit. He looked so handsome as he smiled carrying his bass fiddle. I just ran with the band and sat at another corner table. It is still hard to imagine all that had happened in less than two days.

Father. Rhumba Outfit.

Me and my father.

The next four weeks I was alone most of the time. Dad would disappear in the afternoon, always returning in time to go to the clubs. He never mentioned where he went and I never asked him. He told me the band's name was "Francisco Condes Rhumba Band." The band played after the 11 o/clock News on a Saturday night. They also played one night stands (called "gigs") all over the country.

He took me the next Saturday to "Bentalls" in Richmond. It was an Afternoon Tea Dance. I sat enthralled watching the people dance. I was still trying to fathom what kind of a world I was in. On the way home, he asked me if I thought I could play the percussion instruments in the band. They were called maracas, cabasha, claves, chocla etc. Like a puppet I answered, "I think so." With my dad I practiced the next week. I was a natural. After that week I joined the band for the radio show and the gigs. Never did I play in the two clubs. My life was rushing under my feet. Less than a month and I was on the radio and I had travelled out of town twice.

The trips out of town were exciting: the hustle and bustle; the railway stations full of service men and women going to various postings; very little room on the trains. Watching my dad maneuver his bass fiddle in the crush was very funny to see. Some people obliged and moved out of the way, others scowled at him when he came too close, another time a man yelled, "Watch it, busta." From somewhere my dad had bought two evening dresses which I wore on stage. The problem was they didn't fit me. They had to be pinned on me to make them fit. Also, I didn't wear a brassiere; I had NO idea what a bra was. The girl singer in the band combed my hair up, with curls on top at the front, just like Betty Grable. I was like a puppet, being told what to do, how to do it, and when to do it. After a gig, my dad paid me a pound. All this the first month in London! The people in Haswell Plough would never believe it. I didn't.

When I was alone I used to go and sit on the steps leading up to the flats just to watch the world go by. One day I noticed a girl coming towards me, her hair bobbing up and down; she had trousers on. That was a new sight for me. Service women, movie stars, yes, but not someone close to my age in men's trousers. She stopped and told me her name was Pamela and she lived just up the street. We chatted for a while about nothing in particular when out of her mouth piped, "Do you like to dance?" I replied, "Yes." "Well," she said, "why don't you come with me this Saturday to Covent Garden Dance Hall? It's a shilling to get in and the band is "Ted Heath's Band." I had the money but "Ted Heath" meant nothing to me. With some misgivings, I said, "Yes, OK. I'll meet you here, 6:30 pm Saturday." "TTFN," she said and off she went. What's TTFN? Sure enough, she arrived Saturday 6:30 pm.

I don't remember telling my dad about the dance. Pamela started to fill me in about "Covent Gardens" and all the servicemen from different countries. "Do you jitterbug?" she asked. "No," I answered without saying, what is jitterbug? "Oh well, you'll soon learn. The Yanks are the ones who are great. They fling you all over the place … up in the air, behind them, between their legs. knees twisting," I wanted to go home.

The dances at Grandma's were much safer. The barn dance, quickstep and the waltz. Before we arrived at Covent Garden, she whispered in my ear, "Don't tell anyone I'm Jewish." I wouldn't, I said to myself; why would I? I didn't know she was a Jew. What a strange thing to ask me. Later on I understood the request.

Covent Gardens was most impressive. Because of its size, the inside had been turned into a dance hall to accommodate the masses of service men and women coming into London on leave to be entertained. You knew it was an Opera House as soon as you entered it. They had kept some of the chandeliers. The tiered balconies were a rich red, made of a soft velvety material. There were Yanks sitting in the boxes trying to act La De Da. No alcoholic drinks were served. The walls had chairs placed against them. At the end of the dance floor was a raised stage with a swing dance band playing "Boogie Woogie Bugle Boy from Company B." Like a sponge, I took all of this in.

We paid our shilling and left our coats at the cloakroom. Then we stood hoping someone would ask us to dance. Pamela was asked and off she went to dance a foxtrot. I never saw her again till it was time to go home. An hour later I was asked to dance a waltz by an American soldier. Whew, I knew how to waltz. Watching the jitterbugging was fun. Everyone was laughing and having a great time. It was true the girls were being flung this way and that way. Sometime later, another soldier asked me to dance. Like the first partner, he asked, "Would you like to dance?" Then, never saying anything until the dance was over, he said, "Thank you."

Oh no, a fat airman came for a dance! I said, "No, thank you." I waited and nobody else asked me. The fat airman still wasn't dancing, so I went up to him and said, "I think I will have that dance." The memory of this still haunts me. He began to lecture me on my rudeness and bad manners. One does not refuse a dance because you don't like the look of a person and then go back to that person and say, "I think I will have that dance." I was MORTIFIED and learned a lesson. I never refused a dance again. How gracious he was to dance with me.

So much to learn in such a short time. Another American soldier asked me to dance. The tune was "In The Mood," my first experience jitterbugging. It was exhilarating as I was flung here and there. I don't know if the soldier enjoyed it. Oh, he must have! He asked me if I would like a lemonade. "Yes, please," I said. I waited and waited. I couldn't believe he wouldn't come back until I saw him dancing it up with a smashing older girl. I had had my last dance for the night.

But I did enjoy watching the other dancers and trying to memorize their moves. I've got a lot to learn in more ways than one.

Pamela arrived all hot and bothered. "We've got to move fast or we'll miss the tube home." Now I was looking at Pam's dress (it was 'Pam' now), black and low cut at the front, her hair was wrapped in a snood, and her shoes must have had 2" heels. Also, her makeup was nice. My red dress paled in comparison; too girlish. My flat lace shoes and frizzy hair didn't help. No makeup. I must have looked dowdy. No wonder I only had four dances. "See you Saturday," Pam said as she wished my goodnight. Full of enthusiasm I replied, "Oh yes." That week I danced every night in my dreams. I was ready the next Saturday; hair pinned up, a pair of shoes with a heel that I bought off a barrow in the market. It didn't matter what color and well, the red dress had to do. Pam put lipstick on me and a puff of powder. My confidence was on the rise. With all that I didn't get asked for any more dances. I was learning so much, but I am not sure what.

"Your mother is coming home at the end of the week," my dad said. How did I feel about that? I tried not to worry. I prepared myself for the meeting which was uneventful. "Hello," was her greeting. "I see you have settled in O.K." There was talk about the lovely manor in the country where she was recuperating. Nothing was asked about my life back in London after five years. Did she know where my dad went every afternoon? I had better say nothing in case she didn't. Just try and fit in. That is what I will do. Try and fit in.

My mother, Elsie.

My mother obviously didn't know where my dad was disappearing to each afternoon. She just went to the pub around 1pm till 3pm then again at 7pm till closing at 11 pm. She had her favorites among the many pubs in the area. She would take me with her now and then. I would watch, listen and drink lemonade. Suddenly she announced I was signed up at her hairdressers as an apprentice to learn the trade. I would receive ten shillings a week. I wasn't sure I wanted to be a hairdresser, but at fourteen I had no say in the matter.

Mrs. Rosencranz owned the salon, her daughter, Rosie, was the hairdresser. They were Jewish. I disliked Mrs. Rosencranz from the start. She was fat, bossy and loud. Rosie was kind and patient. The first month all I did was wash basins and sweep up hair clippings. I advanced to rolling hair into metal cylinders and shoving them into electric sockets to perm hair.

My attempt to manicure was a failure; too many cut cuticles from my shaky hands. After my first practice on my dad he said, "I don't think so," as we looked down at the blood.

My big fear was plucking eyebrows. Rosie said, "Make an outline across the brow then all you do is pluck the hairs out underneath, then match the other side." It seemed so easy when I practiced. My first attempt on a customer was a failure. One side never quite matched the other, so I kept on plucking until a mighty scream came from the lady. "She's plucked them all out!" Not quite. Rosie came to the rescue and finished the job.

It was some of the conversations between Rosie and her clients that interested me. The chatted as if I were deaf. This conversation happened just before Rosie was to marry. Client: "Rosie, you do know what to expect?" "No," said Rosie. Whisper, whisper, whisper, followed by gales of laughter. Client: "It's true sometimes you can feel it move around in the night." More laughter. "You're joking!" said Rosie, as the business of the day continued. Client: "Well, all I can say is, I would sooner have it than breakfast any day." My ears were ringing. What moved around in the night? I couldn't imagine … and she would sooner have it than breakfast? I couldn't find an answer for that, so I put it out of my mind.

Mrs. Rosencranz was something else. If the salon was quiet, she would give me other work to do that had nothing to do with hair-dressing. For example: chopping large pieces of wood into smaller pieces for the fire; sweep the extension that connected the salon to the men's barber's shop. Another time I was sent to the Kosher butcher's shop to pick up meat. I watched soft eggs being squeezed out of a fowl.

The last straw on the camel's back for me came in two folds. I heard her telling Rosie about: "It shouldn't have happened, they fell apart in my hands." A couple of weeks later Mrs. Rosencranz asked me if I would like to buy some underpants without coupons. I eagerly said, "Yes." I gave her my ten shillings and received six pairs of un-derpants. A good exchange, except on the first attempt to wash them they fell into shreds!

My mind went back to the conversation I overheard. I was only 14. I was too nervous to say anything. The week of Rosie's wedding I decided to go to the synagogue to see her married. It was all very exciting, especially when a glass was stamped on and everyone shouted with delight. I was so happy that I had decided to attend. It was interesting. When the ceremony was over, I followed the people up stairs where a table was filled with food. How nice. I went over and helped myself to a sandwich. Suddenly, with my mouth full of food, Mrs. Rosencranz was saying in my ear, "What are you doing here? You're not invited." Another voice from Mrs. Rosencranz's oldest daughter chimed in, "Oh for goodness sake, mother, drop it, let her along, it's Rosie's wedding." The damage was done. I shoved the rest of the sandwich in my pocket. My face red, I fled down the stairs and raced back to the flat. I had no idea I had to be invited.

Within two weeks, I left. I'm sure I wasn't missed. Now what, Grandma … where do I go from here?

It was a sunny afternoon, dad was out, and my mother had just come in from the pub. There had been a fearful row between them the night before. I had no idea what it was about. I said to my mother, "I would like to go to the zoo." No reply. I repeated, "I really would like to go to the zoo." She signed, then said, "Oh well, if we must go." She dragged her feet all the way. It wasn't a pleasant visit at all. I was glad to return to the flat.

Entering the living room she stopped abruptly. Following her eyes, I saw on the mantle shelf two envelopes. One was addressed to Jean, the other to Elsie. I never did know what hers contained. Mine was brief and to the point. He (my dad) was leaving for good, to live with May and Derek. He will explain more later (he never did). I started to tremble. He's never coming back. He's leaving me with her. I felt sick. We both looked at each other; not a word was said. I was bewildered and scared. I never understood for the next six months he still taught pupils in the flat. For several years after he left, I still played gigs, made two Decca records, and performed at weddings.

I was now aware of men being around. Late one night there was scuffling. Changes were taking place. I was becoming aware of adult behavior. I would watch and listen. I never questioned anything. I was too frightened. But I couldn't hide the look on my face when she came home drunk. My look drove her mad. Tension was simmering between us.

Dad had been gone a couple of months. One night she came home drunk. She started ranting. I looked at her with disgust and I back talked to her. She screamed, "You black bastard!" I ran out of the room, grabbed my coat, and went to the tube station. There is a music student of my dad's and he knows where my dad lives. I'll go see him. I found his house. He wouldn't tell me where my dad lived but he would go and get him for me. It was dark by now. I saw a church and I sat against its wall in the cemetery. Pulling my knees up to me, I waited over an hour till my dad came. I wasn't afraid in the cemetery, but it was cold. My dad took me back to the flat after I told him what happened. He told me to go to bed. What was said between them I never knew. Once again, nothing was ever mentioned. She smelled of whisky and gin. I told her, "I never asked to be born." That really riled her.

On a good day, so I thought, she took me to a place with lots of music. I thought it was a strange place. There were people dancing. Many of them were dressed like men. One of them came up and asked me to dance. At the end of the dance, I was sure it was a woman. She said, "You're not my type." What was she talking about? I never went there again.

Many years later I learned about lesbians and homosexuals. Looking back, I think my mother was trying to destroy me. Another time, after a donnybrook, she went into the kitchen, locked the door and I heard her put shillings into the gas meter. Why, what is she doing that for? Many years later I knew her mind was dwelt on suicide by gassing herself, or was she being dramatic?

More than once there were scuffles outside our door. Opening to see what it was, a man had her pinned against the wall, or a man was running up the stairs. I didn't like what I saw. My brain was trying to give me information. She would tell dirty jokes or give me written ones which left me with ... 'Can't be a man's thing. No. Adults do that?' My mantra after that was ... O.K., adults do that.

My mother introduced me to a man called Bill Jones. He was 28, he had a limp, the result of Dunkirk (never heard of it). He used to come to the flat. I was not 15. He raped me one night when I was alone with him. I didn't know what was happening, only the terrible pain. I liked him. Another moment of ... this is what adults do. I associated with him for another three years. He used to take me to visit his family. I liked sitting around the table with his mum, sister and brothers.

The house held seven adults and one child. It was crowded. They knew how old I was, but nobody said anything. One week I was so lonely, with no money. I started walking early one morning to visit them in Carsholton over 20 miles away. I got about six miles from Morden and a rain storm started. I sheltered in a doorway with a man who asked me questions. He was astonished when he heard where I had walked from and that I had no money to get to my destination. He gave me two shillings to continue my journey by tube and bus. Was I grateful.

Bill Jones should have gone to prison for what he did to me. I never told anyone until I was in my nineties.

My mother was doing odd work for a tailor. I helped for a week or so but I was hopeless with a needle and thread. I was still doing the odd gig, no regular work, V1s and V2s were dropping all over the place and I was still going to the dance hall, my only escape from my life.

Then I met Cecil, a twenty-year-old merchant seaman. When he was in town, he took me to his home for dinner with his family. One Saturday his five sisters were there all dressed in different military service uniforms. I enjoyed them all.

One weekend leave that Cecil had, I was sick at the dance. He had visited the flat so he knew where to take me. I couldn't stop coughing and I was very hot. He bundled me up and walked to Boots, the chemist, in Piccadilly Circus. They supplied me with some medicine and Cecil put me in my mother's bed. I couldn't sleep on the bed settee because my mother had two friends sleeping there. Cecil left me with a cup of tea. He had to report back to the ship.

My mother arrived home about 11:30 with her two friends (a man and wife). During the night I was crying and saying over and over again, "I feel so poorly." "Oh shut up," she said repeatedly. The next afternoon an elderly doctor came to see me and within the hour an ambulance had whisked me off to St. Mary Abbot's Hospital in Kensington. I was incapacitated for two months, being bed bound the first month.

I had pleurisy in both lungs. If I hadn't been so ill, I would have enjoyed the stay. The care I received from the nurses was wonderful. I was in a ward with eleven other beds. I was the youngest.

Mrs. Giles in the next bed was beautiful. She was very ill. I used to climb on my bed and peep over the screen between us and watch them put needles in her chest. She never moved. She looked so peaceful. Her husband was in an Air Force Officer's uniform. He came to see her a few hours before she died. I was so sad. She had an angel's face.

I often wondered if her husband survived the war. Also, did Cecil come to the dance hall looking for me, not knowing I was in hospital? I still have the cross that he brought me from Jerusalem by my bedside. I feel deeply that he never survived the war. A kind, gentle boy. We were like ships that pass in the night.

My dad sometimes brought Derek to visit me in the hospital. My mother came several times with a friend. She brought Jimmy the Greek who owned a small cafe. He would send eggs in with her and the nurses would boil them for me in the kitchen at the end of the ward. As I look back, Jimmy was a near miss. He invited me up to his rooms above the cafe. I sat down and he touched my shoulders. I looked at him, he stopped, then said, "Let's go downstairs for tea." His conscience stopped any ulterior motive he may have had.

When I came out of the hospital my mother had a girl, Glennis, living with her. I liked her because she was friendly. Glennis was from Merthyr Tydfil in Wales. She was an usher at the Windmill Theatre. I used to get free passes from her to see the shows. This was the only theatre allowed to show nudes. The one stipulation that the government enforced was the nudes did not move. They put tableaux on from famous events in history like "Napoleon's Retreat from Moscow" and "Death of Nelson." One night she came home laughing to tell us an American had thrown a mouse on the stage and all hell broke loose.

The showgirls had to be admired. All through the bombing and rockets the theatre never closed. I am now becoming more aware of this thing called sex. This is what adults do. I never spoke to anyone about this subject. I watched and listened.

One night I was in the flat and a knock came on the door. I opened it and there stood a friend of my parents called Jimmy Clark, standing with his pants down, holding his erection in his hand, and he was laughing. I slammed the door shut. It was the first time I had seen this part of a man's body. I was trembling. What a shock! I was trying to equate this horrible scene with the Jimmy Clark who teased me, played games and laughed with me when I was a child. This incident has stayed with me all my life … horrible!

In my fifteenth year, my dad took me for a singing audition to perform on AFN – American Forces' Network. I was a natural, but an untrained singer … no sophistication or style. When I walked into the room there sat five top American military brass. Not a smile on their faces. My stomach was in a knot. What was my dad thinking?! The pianist took my music. I can't remember what I sang – croaked. I was a flop.

The next audition a week later was for The Cabaret Club on Beak Street. If I was hired I would be part of a trio. Trios were popular then because of the Andrew Sisters. Unlike the clubs of today, The Cabaret Club was "membership only" with a high price. It opened around 10 pm serving dinner. There were two shows, one at 11:15 pm, the second at 1:30 am. Its company consisted of four chorus girl dancers, a solo male dancer and a solo female dancer, plus an exotic dancer. There was a trio singing. The show was centered around a comedian. The club had an eight-piece band.

The format of the shows changed every six weeks. You rehearsed the next show while performing the current one. I passed my music to the pianist at the same time noticing my judges; a large man smoking a cigar, I think his name was Van Dam, and he was with a couple of other men. I was so nervous. I sang, "Don't Fence Me In" like it was a hymn. Olive, one of the trio, said, "Can you swing it?" I did as I was told then sat down and waited. The three men chatted with Olive, who came back and told me I was hired.

Rehearsals started the next week. Before I left the club, Olive said, "You have to change your name; the other girl is called Jean." I changed my name to Claire. Then she said, "You're singing harmony." "What" I said to myself, "is harmony?" I had never heard the word let alone sing it. Was I petrified. I will never know how I got through the rehearsals. I learnt fast and having a good ear for music helped. I managed to wing it. There were no complaints.

At the first dress rehearsal I found I had a problem. I had never undressed before anyone except Grandma. There I was in this small room with all these girls and trying to put my costume on without them seeing my underwear. I was embarrassed when I noticed a couple of the dancers laughing at me. I still stayed as discreet as I could.

"Exotic" meant nothing to me. I had never heard of the word. I knew what it meant after watching, for the first time, our well-built "exotic dancer" dance to "I've got you under my skin" at the same time dropping one veil after another. The seventh veil was dropped a split second with the lights going out. I wasn't sure if I saw her naked body or not. "Timing" is a word in the entertainment world.

I sometimes took a pillow with me to sleep on between shows. The club was 35 minutes from the flat. Whilst walking home one night clutching the pillow with one hand, flashlight in the other, at 3:30 am I became aware of a car following me. Suddenly it went ahead and stopped. Two men got out and approached me. I thought I would die. To my relief, they showed me their Private Police badges. They wanted to know what I was doing out at that time of the morning and what was I carrying. It all sounds so ridiculous now. I showed them my pillow explaining to them where I had come from and where I was going. When they were satisfied with my explanation, they wished me good night and I continued on my way home.

When working with the band, my dad was exciting and fun. Because my father was in the band, I enjoyed a certain amount of protection. As John's daughter I was never harassed. A night club, however, is a different kettle of fish. There can be many pit falls. Later I was to learn that because I looked eighteen or nineteen the club hadn't questioned my age at the time of hiring me. The problem was it was illegal for someone of my age to work in that kind of environment. Obviously my father hadn't told them. Often I've asked myself if I've ever regretted the experience. Always I answer 'no.' Observing the various types of people, listening to the many topics of conversation, and watching their actions forced me to grow up almost overnight, which helped prepare me for what was about to come. These were not bad people, just different from those I had encountered up to that time.

In retrospect, I have talked about The Cabaret Club many times and been asked, "What was it like?" but no one has ever asked me how I felt. I find that interesting. At fifteen I left the club. Now what? I had no money, very little to eat.

A while later I was offered a job in Maida Vale taking and bringing home from school a five-year-old girl called Joy. During the day I did housework or cooked a meal for Yollie, Joy's mum. Yollie was gone all day. This I am not proud of. One day I found a bunch of letters in a drawer. The letters were to Yollie from an airman. They were love letters; nothing ugly, rude or sexual - just how much he loved her, was missing her, and that he may never see her again. I cried and put the letters back. I knew I had read something sacred. Later I found out he had been killed.

I left Yollie's when her husband came to visit Joy every week. He started putting his hand up my skirt and saying, "Isn't it nice?" Once again … this is what adults do.

All this time I am doing gigs with my dad. Living with my mother was getting to be a challenge. As I came out of a shop one day the old man Percy, who slaved at the "Greasy Spoon" restaurant, stopped me and said, "Your mother is an Eire Woman." What did he mean? I knew I had to get a job. I had little money. Grandma's money in my savings account was running out.

My life was no life at all … visiting Bill Jones' family, not much to eat, and being frightened of the doodle bugs. The V1s caused great anxiety. They would chug over our heads and we knew when the chugging stopped that's when they came hurling down. Recently it was announced that a different kind of rocket, a V2, was being launched. This one just flew then hit the ground, no warning at all. This night I was in my underwear putting a cloth over some rhubarb when a mighty explosion went off. I ran from the kitchen grabbing my coat. At the same time my mother was doing the same. The street was in chaos.

For a moment all I could see was the large, gloomy looking church where, in the evenings before the war, I and dozens of inner-city children would go when we had nothing better to do. There the nice, kind ladies would give us crayons, chalk, colored paper, scissors, glue and string. From these we made all sorts of imaginary things. The evenings would finish off with lemonade and biscuits. That memory was now shattered as a flaming wall of the church suddenly, with a grinding roar, crashed to the ground while people screamed and scurried to get out of range to avoid being hit. Transfixed I just stood there watching as others tended to the wounded. Some were crying, most were speechless – including me. Also, I had no idea where my mother had disappeared to.

At first my attention was riveted on the three-storied flats situated on both sides of the church. The various shapes of the rubble that formed as the flats tumbled were enhanced by the brilliant lights from the fires and, except for the absolute terror of the occasion, might even have been considered beautiful.

I slowly became aware of the broken glass I was treading on, and of the bodies I was walking around, when a voice got through to me, yelling, "I need some cloth. Has anybody got a cloth? She's bleeding badly." Hearing this I bent down and, apart from my coat, took off the only other piece of clothing I was wearing – my knickers – and handed them to him. The ambulances from Middlesex Hospital, only a few blocks away, had already begun to arrive on the scene. As I turned away from the chaos, to head home, another voice yelled out, "They need blood donors at the hospital." I immediately changed course and made my way to the hospital.

The injured were everywhere. "Can I help you?" a nurse asked me. "I've come to give blood," was my reply. She asked, "Are you eighteen?" "Yes," I said. She then pointed me in the right direction. I gave blood for the next four years, four times a year, until a doctor, looking at my chart, said, "How old are you?" "Eighteen," I said. He smiled, looked at me, and said, "I think you need a rest, don't you?" That was the last I heard from the hospital.

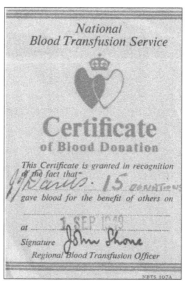

Blood donor certificate.

I needed work. Somebody suggested the Labour Exchange. They sent me to Boots the Chemist on Regent Street; a pound a week and twenty minutes from the flat. Boots was boring, not much merchandise to sell. The manager, Mr. Sills, was kind. He would send me to another Boots to replace absent staff who were either ill or on holiday. I received extra money for this.

At this time I met a very nice American paratrooper from Boston. His name was Louis Coleman. He was a real gentleman. When he had leave, we would meet at the dance hall, Covent Gardens. I only took him to the flat once. He looked around, not saying anything, then he asked where the bathroom was to bathe in. "There's only the galvanized sink to wash in," I said. He shook his head replying, "That's a whore's bath." "What is a whore? I asked. He shook his head again, smiled, and said, "It doesn't matter." I was still at Boots when he returned to the U.S.A. We did write periodically.

Louis with Lilly and me, 1950. Zugspitz, Germany.

right to left, Tommy, Lilly and me.

Paratrooper Louis

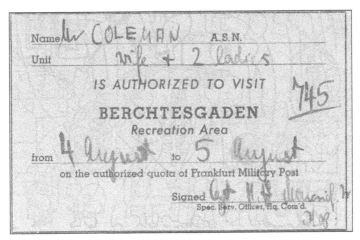

travel document

I now became aware I was very much in the way at the flat, but where do I go? It was at that time a lady representative of Boots asked to see me. She told me Boots had a complex for girls which might be suitable for me. I would live there and have meals. There was a curfew and rules to follow. It sounded OK but I wasn't sure about following rules. I had a month to think about it.

Another session came up with my mother; the usual smell of whiskey as I entered the room. She started on and on. I couldn't stand it. I picked up the scissors and moved towards her. Then my brain kicked in … Grandma's words. "Jean, no matter what your mother does, she is your mother." I put the scissors down, picked up a bottle off the table, and started to hit my head with it. I stared at my mother's confused face. She left the room. A word never was said about it.

Putting my coat on, I went to Tottenham Court Road Police Station and told them I had no place to stay. They sent me to a church army hostel near Edgeware Road. The man in an army uniform heard my plight and showed me to a room upstairs.

The room had eight metal cots. Two were occupied. Later I was sure those women were prostitutes. I lay on one; I never undressed or slept. The bell for breakfast rang at 7:30. The breakfast consisted of a tin mug with tea in it and a piece of bread and margarine. I located the office. Behind the desk sat the weary-faced Army man. He looked up at me as I placed a shilling on the desk and thanked him for helping me. I wasn't going back there. I had no other choice but to return to my mother's flat. Once again, not a word was spoken between us. I missed a day of work.

The next morning I made an effort to look nice. I put lots of curls in the front part of my head, just like Betty Grable. I then put on a red skirt and a yellow sweater. I really looked nice. Later in the day I overheard a manageress say to Mr. Sills, "Have you seen Miss Davis? She looks like a cockerel," and they laughed. I was crushed. She then came to me and said, "Miss Davis, your outfit is inappropriate and too daring." That did it. No way was I going to live in their girls' complex.

The next incident sealed my decision to leave "Boots the Chemist." Every week another girl and I were sent downstairs into the supply area to weigh out soap flakes into 8 oz. bags. As we were working, this girl (I can't remember her name) said, "I was at a big dance last night and the band was fabulous. The band was called ... and the leader was ... ." I had never heard of either name. She went on, "You must know them, after all you've told me!" What am I going to do? If I told her that I had never heard of them, she would think I had been lying, and so I said, "Oh yes, I know the leader and the band." "You bloody liar!" she said. "All those stories of radio shows and a night club, traveling in England ... I knew you were lying." I had put myself in a trap. "I never went to a dance, I made it up," she continued. We never spoke again. This was a turning point.

Thank goodness it is Saturday. Boots the Chemist can be so boring when you have so little to sell. The soaps which had arrived that morning sold out quickly, also the men's razor blades. Sighing, I put the pure boar shaving brushes back in the glass case. Then, after counting the cash and delivering it to the department head, I was off like a shot to the underground train and on my way to my so-called home.

Coming through the door I was informed there was a telegram waiting for me. Tearing it open, I discovered it was from my father telling me my Grandma Mendi was dead and I was to be in Haswell Plough the next day. What was I to do? I didn't have enough money on hand to pay for the train ticket, so I went and asked my landlord if he could help me, and he loaned me the cash.

What a rush, packing what I needed, then dashing across London to King's Cross Station to catch the last night train. All I could think of, sitting in the train going to Durham, was … my Grandma's dead.

Arriving in Durham around 7:00 am the next day, hungry and tired, I waited for the first bus to Haswell Plough. I hadn't seen my father for quite some time. He was waiting for me at Grandma's house.

What an entrance. The same old lumpy furniture. A black kettle sitting on a trivet held over a blazing fire. Most noticeably, Grandma lying in the coffin under the front window. Crossing past my father, I went to see her. Looking down at this bruised and grey face, my thoughts repeated once again … my Grandma's dead. Then I said to myself, "What will I do? She was always there. Now I have no one." No tears. She gave so much of herself to me and I had nothing to give back.

Monday was the funeral. The morning was dark and rainy. People arrived about 11:00 am. Around the corner came a black car for my father and me, followed by (I couldn't believe it!) a double-decker bus. A double-decker bus for about twenty people. If it hadn't been such a sad occasion, I could have laughed!

Thornley Cemetery is a lonely place in the middle of nowhere. Watching Grandma disappear down the hole, I thought, "Now she is with Queenie, her mum who was only fourteen years older than her."

I stayed quiet and listened to the neighbors chatting about "Maggie" (known only to me as Grandma Mendi). One mentioned that Maggie had promised her the pierced earrings that she wore. Another said she was getting Maggie's washing machine. All this going on while laughing, eating cream puffs and drinking beer or lemonade.

That night my father and I went to the pub. He entertained with his guitar. I sat taking it all in. As I was about to leave the pub for the return journey to London, my father pushed the money for the fare into my hand. All I had left of my Grandma were pictures of her and her flower vases.

Explaining my absence from work on the Monday and Tuesday, all I heard was, "That's a likely story."

The next week, the month was up and I told Boots that I wasn't going to their girls' complex. The following week I was fired. I had no job; four pounds to my name and living with my mother, who I had begun to detest.

That same week I found myself at Hammersmith Palais. Whilst I was dancing with this boy and passing the usual, "Do you come here often?" it got around to me unloading on him that I was fired that week and was desperate for a job. He suggested I apply for a position where he worked. "Where abouts is that?" I asked. I couldn't believe my ears when he said, "It is in the West End on Bemers Street."

Bemers Street was a block from my mother's flat, also around the corner from where she was a barmaid. What a coincidence. I went to this firm called Hovendens. It was a hairdressers' wholesalers. The following week I applied for a job and I was told to start in two weeks. The wages were three pounds a week and it was situated in an area I knew well. Now I was in the position to leave the flat. But where to? I began to feel nervous. Was I supposed to stay at the flat because it was close to Hovendens? My mind was in a whirl. I had nobody to talk to. I had no friends. I sat and pondered it out. What does a girl of fifteen do?

I've no idea what made me take a bus over to the south side of London. I walked around Brixton. Looking in the window of a news-agent shop, the only ad for a room to

rent was on Paradise Road, Stockwell Park. It must be a lovely place with a name like that. I made my way to Paradise Road and was surprised to find it badly bombed with only a few houses on it. I found the house, knocked on the door, and a woman answered. She was about the age of my mother. "You'll have to share a room," she said. "That is alright," I replied. Back to the flat I went, packed some things, and returned to Paradise Road at 10 shillings a week.

It had problems; it was only a bedroom. We had permission to use her kitchen for evening snack. I laugh now when I think of this skinny girl coming into the room the first night saying hello, getting undressed and getting into bed in her underwear. Then I followed suit.

Over the next week we began to talk to each other. We did decide this arrangement was not very good. There wasn't anywhere to keep our meager rations. The toilet was in the garden and we had a bucket to use. I knew I didn't want to stay here any longer. My room-mate was Doris and she felt the same. One evening, eating a sandwich in the kitchen, the lady of the house and her children were having supper. I heard a strange noise coming through the ceiling. Nobody else seemed to notice. It suddenly dawned on me it was Doris peeing in the bucket above us. I was mortified. "Got to get out of here," I said to myself.

I told Bill Jones that I didn't want to see him anymore. By this time my dad allowed me to visit him each month on a Wednesday night. This particular night it was getting dark and just before I reached my dad back garden gate, two figures jumped out and attacked me. They hit my body and punched my face as I screamed "Daddy, Daddy!" (I had never called my dad 'Daddy' before. Suddenly my dad's voice shouted, "What's going on here?" The men took off. "The men" were Bill Jones and his brother, Cyril.

Inside the house I was given a cup of tea. A cup of tea cures nearly everything in England but certainly not my bruised body and black eye. My dad took me to the tube station. He was more concerned about the neighbors. The two could have been waiting for me at the other end for all my dad knew. I wasn't asked back to his house again. I told them at work I had a bad fall. I never saw Bill Jones again.

Wonderful; Doris and I found new accommodations in Balham. We stayed two months. It was worse than the one we left! Wonderful again we found a room in Stockwell Park Road. It was just right; a washbasin, a large wardrobe, a table, two chairs and a toilet just outside our door. Not forgetting a small cupboard for our food ration. The bath was upstairs. We were allowed one bath a week, on Saturday mornings. In two weeks, we were ensconced into what we thought of as heaven.

Within six months Doris decided to go back home to the country. I wasn't sorry to see her go. We had nothing in common. Also, I had enough to pay her share of the rent. I felt safer than I had felt since leaving Grandma's.

Over the next three years, I had several boyfriends but I was not promiscuous. I suspect the rape left me with no desire or passion. I did have a couple of sexual encounters but my mantra was, "That's what adults do." My life consisted of work, dance and the movies. Once in a while I would pop into the pub where my mother worked. No idea why I visited her in the pub. I never went back to the flat. Could it be she would buy my dinner for me or was it a deeper need?

Because I couldn't get coal and my room was freezing, now and again I would go to my mother's coal bunker and steal a bag of coal. I stopped doing it after I dropped the bag on the floor of the tube station. All eyes were on me as I scrambled to try and put the coal back into the ripped paper bag. Other times I would put the hot plate on but it was too expensive. Then there were the times I would pile shoes, books or anything heavy that I could pile onto the bed, then I would get into bed and start throwing the things at the cupboard to stop the mice making a noise. It didn't always work but at least I was warm.

Christmas Eve 1942:

I had nowhere to go so I went to Hammersmith Palais. Sitting at the table; the band had just changed places and Paul Rich, the singer in Lou Prager's Band, came and sat with me. The conversation turned to me being alone. He said, "Come to my house in Golders Green and have dinner tomorrow." I went, met his mother and had a nice dinner. We walked in the park with his red setter dog called "Tavarich." I went home thinking, wasn't it kind of him? A Jewish man inviting me, a Christian, for Christmas dinner. I knew he was sorry for me.

My life was going to make a big change in 1949. I had started to go to the Lyceum Dance Hall which had been an old theatre. Now the war was coming to an end. Covent Garden Opera House was closed. It was the usual Saturday afternoon dance. I was sitting at a table waiting for a request for a dance. A voice said, "Can I have this dance?" I looked up and I was immediately aware I was looking at a mature man well in charge of himself. Taller than I, medium build, good looking, open smile and well dressed; "Yes," I said as calmly as possible. We had several dances.

His name was Alan Russell, although later I found his real name was Albert Russell. I saw him at the Saturday dance several weeks in a row. He was a good dancer. The one Saturday he asked me to dinner after the dance. I was taken to an upmarket restaurant. I was impressed and overwhelmed.

The next date was to visit a friend's mews apartment in Gloucester Terrace. I was a little misapprehensive but I went. Alan was nice and I liked him. The flat was one where years ago a horse was kept. Now it had a car in the space. I found out he was thirty and had been a military policeman throughout the war. As I walked up the stairs to the flat, I'm looking at an oar on the wall with a name and "Harrow Rowing Club" on it.

The flat consisted of a small dining room and kitchen, a sitting room, and a bedroom with a bath situated in the corner. Everything was high quality. What kind of person was this Alan Russell to have a friend so rich? He must be rich to have silver

ash trays, cigarette boxes and music which seemed to be piped from the wall. We talked; he mentioned his friend goes to his house in Marlow (wherever that is) at weekends. I was really enjoying everything around me. Also the maturity of this man. I didn't smoke or drink, but I took my first gin and tonic when it was offered. It's not going to hurt me, I thought, so I had a second.

I woke up in bed. What happened to me? I dressed and went and sat in the lovely sitting room. Nothing was mentioned about last night. Alan knew I was of an age to make my own decisions. He didn't know I didn't drink. He didn't know how impressed I was with everything. I think I was quite flattered that he noticed little old me.

He sometimes went to Marlow on the weekend. He always dressed in tweeds for that visit. Yes, I was another "sitting duck," seduced by all these pleasures.

Then Alan told me we were going to visit his mum. I couldn't believe my eyes when we arrived there. His parents lived in a really poor area around the back of Waterloo Station. I think it was called The Peabody Buildings. They were grey, dirty and crowded. He also mentioned he worked at Black Cat cigarette factory. I suspected now that he lived at his parents' home.

His mum was a worn-out dear old Londoner still doing char lady work. One day I actually saw her carrying a bucket and mop coming out of a building on Regent Street. I hid in a doorway so she wouldn't see me. I didn't want to embarrass her. A friend I only met at the dance was a receptionist at Guys Hospital. The doctors often received free tickets for London shows. If they couldn't use them, they would give them to the receptionist. Many times Eileen couldn't use them so she would ring me at work. I never refused. In my lunch hour, I would rush to Guys, pick up the tickets, then after work make my way to Mrs. Russell's and take her to the shows. "My Fair Lady" and "Oklahoma" were two of the shows. She just loved the evening out.

One day Alan's Auntie Mary was visiting; she also was a char lady cleaning in Chelsea. Her stories of some of the upmarket flats that she cleaned really interested me. She said, "Do you want to come with me next week?" The flat turned out to be a huge apartment with a dining table that seated ten. There were plain maroon simple covers over the chair backs. What's under them? I thought. I lifted one up and there was the Royal Emblem. Mary wouldn't tell me whose place it was, obviously, but they were tenants who entertained the Royal Family.

Back to the mystery of the two sides of Alan. He actually phoned me at work to ask me to lunch at a pub on Firth Street with this rich friend. Of course I went and was introduced to a fine dressed elderly man called Derek; perfect gentleman and charming. Going back to work I was floating on air. I am meeting a different area of society. Now I had seen them enter The Cabaret Club but I had never actually spoken to one of the Upper Class. Where does Alan fit in? The answer came the night we sat in Derek's flat talking. Alan is rambling on; he had had too much to drink. I was back to soft drinks. Derek's full name was Lord Naysmith, who owned this mews flat,

a house in Marlow, and also an estate in Ireland. Derek was an upper brass officer in the last war, stationed in Greece at the same time Alan was a Military Policeman. Alan said straight out Derek killed a boy and I covered up for him. I've had many thoughts since then. At that time, the work 'blackmail' never entered my head as I never the word, but I did know a bad thing had happened.

Five months after I met Alan, I was brought up sharp. How come I have not had my period? I don't understand, it is never late. I am not pregnant. I told Alan, he said I was, and he would take care of it. But I know for sure I am not pregnant, I never wanted to be. Big light bulb lit up. How was I to know? I had never talked about or read any books about "This is what adults do." I thought it was a choice to have a baby. This could have happened to me before now.

Alan phoned me at work and we arranged to meet the next Friday at Kennington Station at 6:30 pm. He assured me my condition was going "to be taken care of." How? I never thought to ask him. The first thing he did was give me ten pounds to give to the lady of the house he was taking me to. Then he said, "I will meet you at the corner pub near the tube station." In five minutes we reached the house. All he said was, "See you later," and walked away. I stood looking at the front door for a few minutes before I knocked.

A pleasant looking, middle-aged lady answered. She obviously was expecting me. I gave her the money. Then I followed her into a room where a man and two teenagers were eating. They looked at me and said hello, I replied, then my arm was taken and I was led into a room next door. It was an ordinary sitting room; chairs, a sofa and a sideboard. There were two exceptions - newspapers laid out on the floor and a wire coat hanger placed on the newspapers.

I seemed to be in slow motion when she asked me to take off my panties and lie on the floor of newspapers. "This may hurt a little but try to keep still." What's happening to me? I thought as I was instructed to pull my legs up. She worked on me for a while then said, "Ah, here it is." She had located something. What was it? Her fingers and coat hanger came out and the pain was over. "Go home and rest," she said. That was it.

I walked back to the pub near Kennington Station, ordered a lemonade and sat waiting for Alan. I thought he was going to be there waiting for me. I ordered three lemonades and drank them slowly until the pub closed. By now I was feeling very unwell. The barmaid didn't seem concerned that I sat on my own for so long. As I left the pub, now knowing what to do, there was Alan coming out of the other corner pub. I had been sitting in the wrong pub. He was very angry at my mistake. I couldn't understand why. Years later I realized he was scared and thought something had gone wrong with the abortion.

I didn't know that was what happened to me. I'd never heard the word. Also, it was illegal and I could have died. Alan continued on with, "We are going back to a
different flat, but I will be staying here overnight with you. The other one is being redecorated and Derek has rented this other one."

All this time I am not saying a word. I was numb as I was guided to this new destination. I can't even remember where it was or the layout of it. Suddenly, in the middle of the night, I knew I was in trouble. I found my way to the bathroom and it happened ... a dreadful, frightening experience. So much blood! I thought my inside was leaving me. I was desperately trying to help myself and take control. I was on my own during the entire experience. As I left the flat early the next morning, I realized I was in the Gloucester Terrace area. I made my way to the tube station and went home.

My mind was crazy, trying to figure out what had happened to me. Although I didn't know the word then, I had been "violated." The word "guilt" has never entered my head. Over the years I've felt a deep sadness for the little girl in a gym slip who was thrown to the wolves by irresponsible parents. By the Grace of God I survived.

Two weeks later, Alan phoned and said Derek had invited me to Marlow that weekend. I said, "No, thank you." The phone went dead. I never heard from him again.

It wasn't all over for me. There were repercussions the following two months. The first occurred on a bus ride to Richmond. I was suddenly convulsed in terrible abdominal pain. I knew I was bleeding but didn't know what to do. I became aware that a young man was standing next to me asking, "Is anything wrong? Can I help you?" "I am in pain," I told him. "The next stop is The Thames," he said. "My friend has a river boat and you can rest there."

The boat was near the bus stop. It did not concern me that there were three or four men on the boat. Words were exchanged and I was told to lie on a bed and tea would be brought to me. When I felt better, I could be on my way. Thank goodness I was prepared for that period. Pulling myself together, I thanked them and caught a bus home.

The next month I was fully prepared, but not for the agonizing pain. This happened in Trafalgar Square. I had just had my 'on the street' photo snapped and was on my way to pick them up at the address the photographer gave me. The house was an old three-story maisonette. I was invited in to wait for my pictures. There were several other men busy with other chores. By then I was relieved to sit down. I was in so much pain. I sat there for ages and it was getting dark. One of the men asked me if I would like to have my picture taken in the nude. I was so scared as I answered, "No." He shrugged then said something to the other men and they left and went upstairs.

I sat trying to figure out where this house was. I couldn't. I went and sat in front of the dying fire. I never slept and sat there getting colder and colder until daylight started to appear through a window. I walked out of the house, found myself near Trafalgar Square, and went home. I never saw anything in that room except reels of film on tables and chairs. The men never came back. Later I became aware I had been in the company of homosexual men. It was difficult for me to comprehend that I was still being confronted by this so called adult world, unknown territory. All those dances I accepted led to some dangerous encounters.

The usual Saturday afternoon at the Lyceum. I had been ensconced in my one room for the last two weeks. No money to go anywhere. Now I had money. Pay day was yesterday. It was comforting to be with people. I listened to the music and enjoyed watching others dance. Then a man asked me to dance. He was very pleasant and we chatted together in between dancing together. He mentioned his friends had just got married and were staying at the Savoy and would I like to meet them later on? Knowing the Savoy was just up the street and was a posh, safe hotel, I said yes.

After tea at Lyons Corner House, we walked up to the Savoy. Following him we went a few floors up in the elevator. How does he know where the room is? I'm asking myself as he stops and knocks on the door. He opens the door and I'm saying to myself: What's going on? This isn't a bridal couple. There were two people in bed. My pleasant man said, "How would you like to spend the night as a foursome?" "No, no," I'm saying as I back my way out of the room. I high-tailed it to the elevator and bolted out of the first visit to the upmarket and 'safe' Savoy.

Since fourteen I've had danger all around me. I've escaped so many bad situations. Looking for companionship in the dance halls made me a target for unscrupulous men. Where else can I go? I don't drink or smoke. The one room is a prison. What kept me safe? Could I have a guardian angel watching over me?

Standing at the counter at work, wrapping a parcel, a voice said to me, "How did you cut your lip?" I looked up and it was Louis Coleman standing there, laughing at me. "What are you doing here, all the way from Boston?" I gasped. "I'll meet you after work and we'll have supper, and I'll bring you up-to-date with my life since I was demobbed."

He was over in England on his GI grant to study commercial art then off to Germany to continue. We made a date for the next night to go to the movies. I was thinking about how well we got on together on our dates during the war. In letters to me he asked me to go over to Boston. I hadn't the courage to do that. Afterwards our letters were few and far between. Now he is back in England and I could get smitten with him again. Who knows? This was exciting!

The next day we met for tea and went to see Danny Kay in "Up in Arms." Sitting afterwards in the tube station, waiting for the train, we were chatting about the past. "I think he wants to get serious," I am saying to myself. Suddenly I'm saying, "Here's my train." He said, "Let's wait until the next one. I have something to tell you." The train came, people bustled on and off, all the while I'm agitated. What has he got to tell me? As the train leaves, he looks at me and said, "I'm married, and Tommy (short for the female name Thomasina) is here with me." He went on to say Tommy knew about me and would like to meet me. I was confused. Why didn't he tell me this before? My future "what if" died right there.

The next weekend I visited with them. Tommy and I hit it off right away. There was another couple there, Len and Lilly. For the next year, I enjoyed the friendship of the four. I had somewhere else to go other than the dance hall. Tommy and Lois left for

Germany but the friendship of Len and Lilly was wonderful for me. My mind was starting to mature. It was so refreshing.

Then one day, sitting at the desk at the top of the stairs, musing away, I became aware of a man carrying sheets of plywood up and down the stairs. He looked so vulnerable with his arm widely outstretched. I don't have a clue what came into me but I picked up some paper, made it into a pellet, then placed it in between a stretched elastic band. The next time he was turning to go up the stairs, I let fly the paper pellet which hit the plywood above his head with a "ping." I looked down fast as his head turned. I waited until the next time he passed me and, giggling to myself, let fly again. My head went down as the sound of "ping" hit the air. I looked up and he was standing thinking about it. He continued up the stairs. Here he comes again. With devilish glee, I repeated the onslaught. I was just about to let go, elastic with pellet aimed, when he turned around: his eyes fixed on mine. He gave a wide, open smile and I sheepishly grinned. On his way down he stopped and I tried to explain my way out of my behavior and he laughed. He asked me my name; he gave me his … Ron Gremo.

By the end of the day we had a date to go to the cinema or dance. I chose the Astoria Dance Hall which was on Charring Cross Road. This was a couples' dance hall. I hope he can dance.

Friday night came. Ron and I were to meet at the corner of Charring Cross Road and Oxford Street. As I approached the corner, Ron appeared on the other side of the street. My face fell. He is only my height. "I thought he was much taller," I said to myself. Oh well, he is very good looking.

The Astoria had a nice ambiance and was small enough to be intimate. We didn't dance the first ten or so minutes, just caught up with details about ourselves. The band began to play the popular tune of the day: "It's Magic." We got up to dance. I could hardly contain my emotions. He was an experienced dancer, skillfully guiding me into the intricate steps of the foxtrot. I thought I had died and gone to heaven! He also recognized that I was no slouch in dancing. We bonded right away. We started dating twice a week, alternating between a movie or a dance.

Walking down the stairs one day in Hovingden's, going for my lunch, I was pulled up shortly with, "What is he doing here?" It was my father coming in the front door. He saw me and joined me on the stairs. He explained that he was short of cash and could I help? We went to the Post Office and I gave him the amount that was the allowed withdrawal for the day. I never gave it much thought. It was the only time this occurred.

A day or two later, I was called into the office of Mr. Morgan, the General Manager. He bid me sit down. I chose to stand. He was a well-built man, always in a business suit, and he had a kindly face. He started with, "Miss Davis, it has been brought to my attention that you were seen on the stairs talking to a middle-aged black man. I am telling you for your own good; that is not the kind of company a nice girl like you should be seen with. I'm sure you agree." I stood still, looking at him and, in a firm voice, said, "Mr. Morgan, that elderly black man is my father." You could have knocked Mr. Morgan down with a feather as his body language crumpled, his voice spluttering his apologies whilst his face turned red. He had no escape except to say, "I am sorry, Miss Davis." With a faint nod of my head I left his office.

A week or so later, I was called into the office of Mr. Jarvis, part-owner of Lovenden's. He is an old man of about sixty five. He asked me to have lunch with him the following day to discuss business. I was thrilled about this because it meant a change in my position. Being a sales girl was all I had ever worked at. We went to an up-market restaurant on Charlotte Street. It was a pleasant lunch with many questions being asked of me ... my background, who did I live with, and where? The only mishap was putting my fork into a pork chop and it shot off the plate. In my confusion and apologies, I knocked over the water glass. Mr. Jarvis was gracious and put me at ease At the end of the week, there was an extra pound in my pay envelope.

I was called into Mr. Jarvis' office the next week. He smiled and mentioned the pleasant lunch. Then he beckoned me to the side of his desk. As I walked closer, his hand went up my dress and panties. He opened the drawer and I'm looking down at pink camiknickers. All the time he is asking, "Do you like them? There's more where they came from," also adding I could have a nicer place to live. I never said a word. I was gobsmacked. I left his office with his words "think about it" in my ears. My mind was saying, "What a dirty old sod. I'll never be an old man's darling or a young man's slave." This is a man who had passed my desk every morning with neither a look nor a word. What has made the change? Information about my black heritage from Mr. Morgan.

At the end of the week, off I went to Osborne & Garrett, Hovenden's opposition. I met with Mr. Garrett and asked for a job. When he knew where I worked, he said he was sorry but they didn't hire each other's staff. I went back to Hovenden's and gave them a week's notice. I told nobody why I was leaving. I returned to Osborne & Garrett and told Mr. Garrett I no longer worked for Hovenden's and I was hired at two pounds more than I was getting at Hovenden's. A better job.

I've left Hovingden's. Summer was approaching and Ron asked me if I would like to visit him for a week in Whitstable where his family lived. He would stay with his brother, I with his sister. Naturally "yes" was my answer. To my delight and dismay, Tommy and Louis wrote and invited me to visit them in Frankfurt, Germany with our friend Lilly Jones. I decided to split my two weeks holiday. Although marriage was not in my find at that time, I didn't date anyone else.

Lilly arrived in Frankfurt two weeks before me. I travelled the beginning of August 1950 on my own. Tommy and Louis lived in the American zone of Germany. We had a marvelous first week. Dancing at the commissary, boating in the Apsis. I bought from a German lady some material, for a carton of cigarettes, and the same lady made me a beautiful dress for another carton of cigarettes.

It was sad to see the damage to the city of Frankfurt from our bombs. I put it out of my mind when I remembered London and their bombs. There was a nice boy, Gerhard, who wanted to date me but I couldn't bring myself to date a German. I was having so much fun I wrote and told Ron Gremo I was staying the next week in Germany.

That week we travelled into Heidelberg and through Bavaria and climbed the base of the mountains. I had never felt such freedom. I felt alive. Louis drove the four of us back to England via Belgium. I had never known such feelings. Brussels, Bavaria, Zugspitz, Frankfurt … I felt I was a "woman of the world."

When I returned to England, Ron was pretty cool towards me, after standing him up, but "absence makes the heart grow fonder." No passion, no desire disappeared. Ron was quiet, consistent and he loved me – me! As our feelings for one another grew, he kept urging me to find a room closer to where he lived. I wasn't sure and dragged my feet. My world was moving so fast, but I was in a trusting relationship with Ron.

Everything was taken out of my hands. My landlord was a kind and helpful person; cups of tea and a biscuit left at my door on Saturday morning bath time. This particular morning, preparing to go upstairs to the bathroom, I made a quick move to go to the door. I opened it and, what do you know, my landlord was on his knees looking through the keyhole! He couldn't get up fast enough as he staggered backwards. If it hadn't been so horrible, the scene could have been funny. This I told to Ron and I was out of Grantham Road in four weeks. Best laid plans of mice and men … new job, new accommodation, and I'm in love.

Life for me was heavenly. My new accommodation was in a large old home with a garden which my room overlooked. There were three other lady tenants and we shared a kitchen. It was nearer to Ron and he was allowed visitation on Saturdays. We decided to get engaged but rings were so expensive with 100% purchase tax. Standing outside a pawn shop whilst waiting for a bus, I looked in its dirty window and there it was, a ring with two diamonds and three sapphires tucked amongst a lot

of junk. I told him about it and we went to the shop to see it. I loved it, especially when the owner said he had had it since before the war and its vintage was around 1910. Ron bought it for fifteen pounds.

At this point, as we were now engaged, I decided to tell Ron about my mulato father. (This is the name used then to describe someone who has half white, half black.) He brushed it off with the words "it didn't matter, he wanted to marry me." Now the word "marriage" had entered the situation, I told him about Alan and the abortion. He was sympathetic and looking at me said, "These things don't matter. I want to marry you." Now I thought my life had become unbelievably wonderful.

A few months later, Ron said his mother was coming for a day's visit. It was obvious she was coming to sound me out. Meeting her at the station I saw a plump, short lady coming towards us with a very open smile on her face. We went to my room for lunch. Although it was six years since the war had ended, we were still on rations. To complement my meager rations, Ron went out to see if there was any fish to buy. Whilst he was away, she made it known that she knew all about me. She didn't sound overly impressed as she self-consciously tried to have a conversation. Finally I said, "Mrs. Gremo, Ron loves me and nothing will stop us marrying."

I found out very quickly Mr. Gremo was a bus driver, she had been born in Lambeth in "the cut" (a very poor part of London) and her life had been one of hardship. I felt pity for this lady sitting next to me on the couch. I thought, "What else am I going to learn?" when Ron arrived with some fish. Conversation ended. We ate some lunch. I watched my month's rations slowly disappearing. Afterwards, we took her to see a movie then to Lions Corner House for tea. We parted on friendly terms. We waved as I saw my future mother-in-law get on the train. My mind questioning around her life; little or no education, abusive husband, son killed in the war, and mother to five children. A sad first meeting.

We then decided to marry early 1952 but there wasn't a flat or anywhere to live. The bomb damage was so vast. "Let's emigrate," I suggested. I had an address in Canada which I found in a letter when I went through Grandma's trunk after she died. The letter was from the son of Grandma's half-sister, Georgina, who was picked up off the streets of North Shields. She was badly neglected and was placed with the Dr. Banardo's orphanage. They in turn sent her to Canada. I knew nothing more about this until I made enquiries to Dr. Banardo's after I came to Canada.

I knew my background was "poverty" but Grandma's and Great-Grandma's was "destitute poverty." There is a big difference. Grandma was poor but we were clean, the rent was paid, clothes were darned, food though it be little was in our stomachs. These things gave you dignity. To be "destitute" meant the workhouse, soup kitchens, sleeping on the streets and rags for clothes. Little Georgina was ten when she came to Canada. Great-Grandma never saw her again. I did meet her.

My life took another turn. When Mr. Ochiltree heard we wanted to emigrate, he discussed it with Mrs. 'O' and they said, "Why don't you apply to the Canadian embassy and if you are accepted for emigration then look for a ship to take you to Canada? When you find one you can then get married and stay with us." Within six months we set our marriage date for March 22nd, 1952 and planned to leave for Canada on October 30th.

I had nobody to assist me the day of my wedding. First I packed what I had in a suitcase, then put my wedding outfit in the hallway with the suitcase. After that, I cleaned the room thoroughly. Next I walked to the hairdresser's to have my hair set, followed by going and picking up my corsage. I wasn't happy when they told me they couldn't get primroses but made a corsage of daffodils. I then walked back to my lodgings, had a bath, got dressed and threw in the trash the clothes I had taken off.

I walked to the bus stop and caught the bus to the church in Crouch End. I didn't want to get off outside the church and chose to walk from the previous stop. I had my suitcase and handbag to carry. Passing a shop window I noticed a very nice tablecloth. I went in and bought it. Sorry, I forgot to mention … as I got off the bus, the conductor said, "Blimey, looks like you're going to a wedding, all dolled up." The daffodils looked like trumpets sticking out from my lapel. As I arrived at the church, Mr. 'O' came running up to me. "I thought you were never coming," he said. After putting suitcase, handbag and new purchase on a seat, I took his arm was walked down the aisle.

Wedding photo. Ron and Jean Gremo.

The church held around seven hundred people. My wedding party consisted of fifteen people. There was no organ playing, only the sound of my shoes hitting the stone floor. It seemed forever to reach the altar. Because I bought my shoes on the black market, I hadn't until later noticed one was blue and one was black! Leaving the church I heard the Rev. Chesney ask, "Anyone got a fag?"

The wedding party proceeded to walk the two blocks to Mr. & Mrs. Ochiltree's where they gave us the reception as a wedding present. Len and Lilly gave us the extra rations as their wedding present.

Two things, one funny and one sad, happened before the day was over. The first; Ron's mother said to me whilst I was coming down the stairs, "I know why you are going to Canada. You're frightened of having black babies in England." I said nothing. The second was ten minutes after Ron and I got into bed. The whole bed fell down! We spent the night on the floor. Seven months later we left for Canada.

Jean Gremo. Passport photo.

Printed in the USA
CPSIA information can be obtained
at www.ICGtesting.com
JSHW072001301124
74461JS00003B/4